WITHIN THE SYSTEM

My Half Century in Social Security

WITHIN THE SYSTEM

My Half Century in Social Security

Robert J. Myers

with
Richard L. Vernaci

ACTEX Publications
Winsted, Connecticut

Manufactured in the United States of America

10 9 8 7 6 5 4 3 2 1

Cover Design by MUF

Library of Congress Cataloging-in-Publication Data

Myers, Robert Julius, 1912-
    Within the system : my half century in Social Security /
Robert J. Myers.
        p.   cm.
    Includes index.
    ISBN 0-936031-12-3 : $19.50
    1. Myers, Robert Julius, 1912-   .   2. United States.
Social Security Administration—Officials and employees
—Biography.   3. Social security—United States—History.
I. Title.
HD7125.M92A3 1992
368.4'3'092—dc20
[B]   92-26776
                                                             CIP

ISBN: 0-936031-12-3

INTRODUCTION

I know what title *I* would give to this wonderful book. To wit and namely, *The Autobiography of a National Treasure.* But precisely because Robert J. Myers, henceforth Bob, *is* a national treasure, the thought would never occur to him. His purpose is simply to convey important information, as far as possible in statistical, which is to say, verifiable terms. Hence, *Within the System: My Half Century in Social Security.*

He does so with the easy, unassuming clarity with which he helped shape and then guide the single most important domestic program of the Federal government from its beginnings far back in the century to this very moment. To this moment, that is, when the chairman of the Subcommittee on Social Security and Family Policy of the Senate Committee on Finance finds himself sitting at a typewriter with the Capitol dome over his right shoulder, bright with late summer sunlight, asking, ''Let's see now. Is Bob to lead off the next hearing on the 'notch?' Let us hope. He is the only one who will tell us the truth. Before the election, at all events.''

The "notch?" These are persons born in the years 1917-1921. When they reached age 65 they found they were receiving somewhat lower Social Security retirement benefits than those in the cohort immediately preceding them. This seems an injustice and a national movement has been organized to redress it. Just Thursday an effort to do so in the Senate failed on a tie vote 49-49. The fact of the matter is that owing to an error in the Social Security Amendments of 1972, those born in the years immediately preceding the "notch babies," as they are known, and who worked well beyond age 62 are receiving higher than intended benefits. This was corrected in the Social Security Amendments of 1977 for those born after 1916, but in a manner that makes many perceive an injustice. As Bob Myers explains in Chapter One, it is nothing of the sort. It is merely that the "bonanza babies" make it seem such. On Thursday we agreed to a Presidential Commission, and perhaps it will come to that. Yet another complicated Social Security issue.

And here is the autobiography of a man who was literally present at the creation. In the summer of 1934, at the very bottom of the Great Depression, what for many seemed the death agony of capitalism, Franklin D. Roosevelt established a Committee on Economic Security, headed by his Secretary of Labor, the incomparable Frances Perkins, to work out a system of social insurance that would provide, among other things, retirement benefits far into a future that, as I have said, many doubted would come to pass. It was the Roosevelt touch. Amazing how the future takes care of itself when folks have a stake in it.

The work of the committee was directed by a gentle giant of an intellect, Professor Edwin Witte of the University of Wisconsin. Robert J. Myers, age 21, signed on as an actuary. In a matter of months, at a cost of $145,000, the group created what is now the largest insurance system on Earth. They did so with astounding accuracy, given the data and data processing resources of the time. Thus, they projected that in the year 1990 some 12.65 percent of the population would be at least 65 years old. The time came round, as time will do. Answer: 12.49 percent. And they did some things as some things have to be done, which is to say, without rhyme *or* reason. What should the retirement age *be*?

In Imperial Germany of the 1880's, Bismarck's social security program put the retirement age at 70. Dr. Francis E. Townsend of California, with his millions of followers in 1934, put the age at 60. Split the difference: call it 65.

The legislation was enacted in 1935; Bob Myers joined the system, rising steadily to the all-important position of Chief Actuary. For all the skill and care that had gone into the legislation, somehow Social Security never found a secure place in American politics. The contrast with the British experience, and of course, the Canadian, is instructive. Social insurance in Britain has been largely the work of members of the Liberal Party, which is to say, persons associated with, and approving of, business and entrepreneurial enterprise generally.

Unemployment insurance, which came to the United States in the Social Security Act of 1935, was passed through the British Parliament in 1911 under the auspices of Winston S. Churchill, then a member of a Liberal government. Similarly, the "cradle-to-the-grave" proposals of the Beveridge Commission of 1942 were the work of a Liberal statesman, Sir William Beveridge. Not so in the United States.

From the outset, elements of the Republican party were either in opposition or suspicious. Bob Myers, a lifelong unashamed Republican (as all actuaries ought to be!), puts the matter plainly enough.

Republicans have always been tarred with the brush of being enemies of Social Security. The system has had its enemies, and they have tended to be Republicans, but that doesn't mean all Republicans — or even most of them — want to destroy Social Security, to hack it out by its roots.

As, indeed, they do not. A Democrat, I have served in two Republican cabinets, and absolutely so affirm. On the other hand ... well, let Bob Myers tell the tale.

Chapter One. ''Heading for Disaster.'' The system had got itself into actuarial trouble, and a new administration saw this as an opportunity to start dismantling the whole enterprise.

This crisis gave the Reaganites an excuse to slice into the belly of Franklin D. Roosevelt's most enduring legacy and tinker with its guts. Social Security was flat on its back and, God help it, the system was at the mercy of people who didn't like it or understand it. Reagan himself in 1964 had gone around the country calling for making the system voluntary. That would destroy it because the low-cost people would opt out, leaving only the high-cost ones in.

And now, his budget director, David Stockman, an owlish, arrogant former congressman from southern Michigan, was ready to wield the knife for him. It was to be the President's first colossal defeat, and according to Stockman himself, it would help stop the Reagan revolution ''dead in its tracks.''

''This was truly the triumph of politics,'' Stockman would later complain in his book bearing that as its title.

This defeat was indeed the triumph of politics. The system did work.

The system was running out of money to pay benefits. The Administration sent a message to Congress proposing to deal with this by fierce cuts in benefits for the lowest income recipients. Cutting expenditures is nothing new to government. If anything, it doesn't happen often enough. But cutting insurance benefits, benefits stipulated in a contributory pension plan, is a very different thing.

The Administration proposal was sent to Congress in May of 1981. Ont he morning of May 20th, I went to the floor of the Senate and offered a somewhat fiercely-worded resolution declaring this would never be allowed. I lost by one vote in the new Senate with a new Republican majority. Whereupon Senator Bob Dole, the chairman of the Finance Committee, which is responsible for Social Security, offered substantially the same measure with the language toned down. I was a co-sponsor. The measure passed 96-0. The crisis wasn't over, but the basis for resolving it had suddenly revealed itself. A third of a century after it was founded, Social Security was becoming a bipartisan program, which both parties would protect.

That this took so long, and that the process is still not completed is as much the fault of liberal Democrats as of conservative Republicans, although for reasons that would (and do) puzzle those involved. As Bob Myers points out, from the very first the "vast, new bureaucracy would be colonized by like-minded people, including men like Wilbur Cohen and Robert M. Ball." These were wonderful people.

I counted the late Wilbur Cohen, later Secretary of Health, Education, and Welfare, as the closest of friends; we served in both the Kennedy and Johnson Administration. Bob Ball is as wise a counsellor as any Senator will ever know; a man of principle, strength, and at the same time, admirable flexibility. They, too, made their mark on American social history. They had, as Bob Myers writes, "from the beginning ... a largely unwritten, but deeply ingrained ... plan that the program would be expanded, that it would evolve as time and circumstance and money would allow.''

The only problem with this ''plan'' was that it was an insider's affair. It had a base in the labor movement, but even there it was the labor movement of the 16th Street headquarters of the AFL-CIO, across the park from the White House, more than the labor movement of the hiring halls. Being insiders, the liberal bureaucrats knew the system was basically sound. What they did not know was that people paying into the system weren't at all sure of this.

Indeed, as I write, a majority of non-retired adults *do not think that Social Security will be there when their "time" comes.* This has made it possible for politicians on the right to denounce the system with relative impunity. If you want to call President Reagan a man of the right, he would be an example, calling as he did in 1964 for a voluntary system, which in effect was no system. It became cost-free for figures such as David Stockman to dismiss the nation's most important domestic program as a ''Ponzi scheme'' and ''closed Socialism.'' Predictions of bankruptcy — lies — caused little resentment, as so many thought they already knew that.

More recently politicians on the left — I think of former Governor of California, Jerry Brown — have not hesitated to propose revising the tax code in a way that would do away with Social Security payroll contributions, and thus abolish the fiscal — and contributory — basis for the entire Social Security program. Again, since it won't be there when the time comes anyway, what is lost by getting rid of it now?

The plain fact is that the Guardians of Social Security made almost no effort to share their information with the American people. To this day, for example, the Social Security Administration *does not want* to send out an annual statement to contributors.

Savings banks send out monthly statements. For the SSA, whose computers are in fine shape, the largest cost would be the postage stamp. But is just doesn't sink in.

There has been another, ironic, cost. The greatest failure of social insurance in the United States has been the provision for dependent children, which is to say, welfare. Welfare benefits (Aid to Families with Dependent Children) are not set on a national basis, and are not indexed. Since 1970, they have dropped by more than one-third in value. In the meantime, the proportion of children depending on AFDC at some point in their childhood has grown to almost one-third. In 1969, President Nixon proposed to change all this by establishing a guaranteed income for everyone.

It was known as the Family Assistance Plan, and was the boldest "expansion" of Social Security ever dreamed of. Alas, it had not been dreamed up by the "expansionists", who hated "the Visigoth in the White House," as they viewed Nixon, or at least many did. To cite Myers, "They abhorred Nixon and were blatant about it." And so the Family Assistance Plan died. That was 1972. We have known nothing but *contraction* ever since.

Most recently, a commission established by the Administration has proposed an increase in the Supplemental Security Income benefit — SSI — a guaranteed income for the needy aged, blind and disabled, the one portion of the Family Assistance Plan that was enacted. That noble former Secretary of Health, Education, and Welfare Arthur S. Flemming, chairman of the commission, comments as follows in his introductory statement:

[W]e fail ... to coordinate SSI and AFDC in an effective manner in spite of the fact that they are both Social Security programs — both committed to lifting the poor out of poverty. President Nixon was right when he urged an income floor for all Americans.

But it is too late for that. Not that we might not be able to afford it, but rather that we could not possibly imagine doing so. That has been the great change in American social policy that began in the 1980's. But that too will change. And when it does, thanks to such as Bob Myers, Social Security will still be there.

Washington, D.C.   Daniel Patrick Moynihan
September 12, 1992   United States Senate

CONTENTS

To my wife, Rudy

CHAPTER ONE

HEADING FOR DISASTER

I had a dirty little secret, and I was praying that no one was going to ask about it. I'd have to tell the truth, and this wasn't a good time for that.

It was 1981. The Reagan Administration had just come into office, and in one swift move it was trying both to save Social Security and, to some extent, pillage it while sticking a knife in the back of the poor. This wasn't the Administration's finest hour. The move was dumb and wrong and was so clumsy that even the Republicans in Congress didn't want to have anything to do with it.

I had to defend the proposal, as the politically appointed Deputy Commissioner of Social Security.

This was September 1981, and the Social Security system was less than two years away from total collapse. By 1983, the retirement and survivors fund expected to be losing $47 million a day if nothing were done to the law. The fund would be losing between $104 million and $153 million a day by 1989, according to figures from the Office of the Actuary of the Social Security Administration.

To put this scary statistic another way, that's a loss of between $72,000 and $106,000 a minute. That's just a few seconds more than the time it's taken you to read this far.

It wasn't going to get to that point, though. The law wouldn't let Social Security go into the red, so when the money ran out, the checks were just going to stop. This has never happened. I trust that it never will, but on that day in September we were headed for it like a runaway stagecoach.

This crisis gave the Reaganites an excuse to slice into the belly of Franklin D. Roosevelt's most enduring legacy and tinker with its guts. Social Security was flat on its back and, God help it, the system was at the mercy of people who didn't like it or understand it. Reagan himself in 1964 had gone around the country calling for making the system voluntary. That would destroy it because the low-cost people would opt out, leaving only the high-cost ones in.

And now, his budget director, David Stockman, an owlish, arrogant former congressman from southern Michigan, was ready to wield the knife for him. It was to be the President's first colossal defeat, and according to Stockman himself, it would help stop the Reagan revolution "dead in its tracks."

"This was truly the triumph of politics," Stockman would later complain in his book bearing that as its title [14][1].

This defeat was indeed the triumph of politics. The system did work.

I say this as a lifelong Republican. But my adult life has been spent building and refining the Social Security system. I went to work for Social Security in 1934, when it had no name and only a handful of employees and was little more than a glimmer behind Roosevelt's pince-nez. I believed in this system

---

[1]This, and other cited works, are referenced on pages 251-52.

and its basic fairness. But right now the question was survival, not fairness.

So I sat in a hearing room in the Longworth House Office Building across the street from the Capitol that September morning and waited for Chairman Jake Pickle to start the interrogation. I had decided to hunker down and hope for the best. Pickle, a Democrat from Austin, Texas, is smart and tough, but fair.

This hearing before his Ways and Means Subcommittee on Social Security could have turned into a lynching. The subcommittee had asked Health and Human Services Secretary Richard Schweiker to testify, along with Stockman.

At the time of the hearing, I was Deputy Commissioner of Social Security, but I had served more than two decades as Social Security's Chief Actuary (from 1947 to 1970). The actuary is the fellow who would tell the higher-ups whether this, the largest insurance system in the world, was on solid financial ground as it tried to take care of this nation's widows, orphans, elderly, and disabled. A good way to think of this is that if Social Security were the Starship Enterprise, I was Scotty. Down in the engine room, I would be listening to the purr of the machinery and reporting to the captain.

Over the years, I had testified dozens of times before Congress, and I liked these people. I think that they liked me back because I always told them the truth, and they didn't have the heart to beat me up.

The best evidence of this came up just a couple of weeks later, when I was testifying before the House Select Committee on Aging, which also was holding hearings on this subject.

The chairman, Philip Burton, looked down at the witness table and tried to put me at ease.

"I am sure you understand that the questions you will get asked and the hostility that may be expressed is not directed at you personally, but at the policies you get a chance to defend," he said.

Burton, a Democrat from California who died a couple of years later, was one of the most foul-tempered and foul-mouthed men in Congress. So for him to say, in effect, "no hard feelings," was a real testimony to my relationship with Capitol Hill.

Anyway, the kind of warmth I had cultivated over the years may have been one of the reasons that the Administration sent me up to the Hill that September morning to testify before Pickle's panel.

Members of the subcommittee could not hide their disappointment that I was the one dispatched to talk to them. Pickle had barely put down his gavel before Andy Jacobs, a plain-speaking Democrat from Indiana, was asking why the big fish didn't show up.

"Was the secretary busy?" Jacobs asked. "What was the problem there?"

Pickle turned to me. "Mr. Myers, can you answer that?"

"Mr. Chairman, I cannot answer that specifically," I replied. "As I understand it, the secretary had another engagement, and I was asked to testify."

That was pretty lame, but the excuse that came from Stockman's office was breathtaking. They said that they lost the invitation. Well, then, they were asked to send something in writing. They couldn't get around to that either. They may as well have said the dog ate their homework.

Jacobs wasn't fooled.

"I think it is reasonable to assume that if the director of the budget took some pride in the Administration's Social Security proposals, even if at the last moment he finally refound our letter, he might have been here," Jacobs said.

He was probably right, but where and why the big boys were hiding out was just a side issue.

By September 1981, Congress, including this subcommittee, was in the final stages of tearing apart the Administration's plan to "save" Social Security. Reagan's plan, or rather the one that his people put forward, had some good elements to it. The plan had eight major points, but two of them were real klinkers.

One was going to slash the benefits paid to people who retired between ages 62 and 65, and the other was going to cut down the benefits of people receiving the minimum benefit.

This was a lousy way to try to get out of a financial mess that, in all fairness, was not of Reagan's making. This one went back to the Carter Administration, the last time someone tried to save Social Security.

In the mid-to-late 1970's, the system was being crushed by the pressures of a recession and high inflation. In 1977 legislation, Congress brought in more money by adjusting the tax rates and expanding the earnings base on which those taxes are imposed. At the time I was serving as a consultant to the House and Senate committees charged with crafting the legislation. They were trying to strike a delicate balance because nobody was wild about the idea of raising taxes.

Carter, in fact, had campaigned for the White House in 1976 by saying that he was opposed to any increase in the taxes to pay for Social Security or Medicare in the near future. He was really boxed in. The House apparently was sympathetic to the new President's dilemma, and its version of the bill had only a small boost in the tax rate between 1978 and 1980 (only 0.2 percent each on the employer and the employee). The Senate version raised the tax rate slightly more, and this was what eventually became part of the law.

Carter swallowed this pill, hoping later to cut income taxes before the next election so that voters would not feel the pinch in their paychecks.

On the morning of December 20, 1977, President Carter stood in the Indian Treaty Room of the Old Executive Office Building next door to the White House for the ceremony to sign into law the changes that he, the Congress, and even I thought were going to keep the system on a sound financial footing.

Boy, were we wrong!

"This legislation is wise," the President said. "It's been evolved after very careful and long preparation. It focuses the increased tax burdens, which were absolutely mandatory, in a way that is of least burden to the families of this nation who are most in need of a sound income."

The President went on to outline some of the major changes: raising the taxes on the highly paid, eliminating sex discrimination, and raising the amount of money which a retired person can earn and still collect Social Security.

"The most important thing, of course, is that without this legislation, the Social Security reserve funds would have begun to be bankrupt in just a year or two, by 1979," the President said. "Now this legislation will guarantee that from 1980 to the year 2030, the Social Security funds will be sound."

Not quite so!

We had misjudged the economy. Instead of getting better, it continued to sink, and the result was that by the end of the 1970's, it became clearer and clearer that the trust fund for retirement and survivors benefits was going to run out of money. The other leg of Social Security, the fund that pays the disabled, was doing all right.

The 1977 amendments had been based on the assumption that economic times would be pretty good in the years immediately following. So for the first four years the financing would be changed just enough to get the system through and build up the fund slowly. The taxes would be increased in the more distant future. This was to defer the pain.

The trust funds are sort of savings accounts, the financial cushion that ensures the solvency of the system. Thus, even if revenue were to be cut drastically by a depression, Social Security could continue to operate for a while.

In 1947, the retirement and survivors fund was a little less than a half-year's outlay, which was a fair margin of safety.

Really, I would prefer that the fund build up to a higher level, say 75 percent or even 100 percent of a year's spending, which is about where it is today.

After the 1977 amendments were law, unemployment went up, inflation was in double digits and wages were rising by only 9 percent. The system was just too finely balanced and too heavily dependent on the forecasts of an improving economy, which, in all fairness, did not seem to be an unreasonable assumption at the time. The worsening of the economy was a blow that it couldn't stand.

The disability fund was in good shape. The actuarial projections made in 1981 showed it not only solvent, but building up a sizeable balance over the next decade. By the end of 1990, it would have between $161 billion and $170 billion, depending on what happened to the economy during those years.

A big reason for this growth was that the fund wasn't paying out as much money as it might have according to earlier estimates. Fewer people were deemed to be disabled, and more people were terminated from the rolls. This was because legislation in 1980 had tightened things up by cutting the maximum benefit paid to the family of a disabled worker (applicable only to future disability cases and not to those then on the rolls). The way that the law had been previously worded, the disabled worker's family could, in some instances, be drawing practically as much money in payments from the government as it had been when the breadwinner was pulling down a paycheck.

In an era of joblessness, which is where we found ourselves at the time, this could effectively keep someone on the government dole. There was little financial incentive to announce that you had gotten well, give up the disability check, and go out to look for a job that probably wasn't there.

In other areas, though, the Reagan Administration was too zealous in kicking what it thought were malingerers off the disability rolls. (The pendulum now is swinging back the other way.)

It didn't take long after that signing ceremony by President Carter in the Indian Treaty Room to see that the 1977 rescue package wasn't going to work. In a couple of years, it was obvious that we'd have to rescue it again.

The economic ice was just too thin, and it left us with too little margin for error. I would have liked to have seen it stronger and thicker. However the assumptions about what the economy might do in the next few years seemed reasonable. And besides, there were other changes being put in the law, changes of a fundamental, social nature, such as eliminating virtually all elements of sexism in the payment of benefits. That, frankly, seemed at least as important as getting Social Security's financial house in order.

Other drastic changes in 1977 involved altering the method of computing benefits. In this case, another fat mistake was written into the law: the ''notch babies.'' These are the 6 million people born in 1917-21 and now alive, whose benefits may, in some cases, be substantially less than those of people with similar earnings records who were born before then.

Most people do not realize — and the notch-baby advocates do not admit — that this inequity does not affect all of the 6 million people, but rather only the minority who worked well beyond age 62 at substantial earnings. Actually, it is not that some notch babies get too little in benefits, but rather those born before 1917 who worked well beyond age 62 get too much, and can accurately be called ''bonanza babies.''

Congress created this notch-baby problem by trying to fix another, very important one that had made benefits too big, and increasingly so over the years.

I had seen the notch-baby problem coming and had warned against it in testimony before congressional committees. I didn't do it as loud as I probably should have. My feeling was we needed to get the law through. If 90 percent of it was good and 10 percent was bad, we'd come back and fix the 10 percent later.

Congress is normally very responsible and careful when it comes to working with Social Security. In 1977, though, it was just trying to do too much at one time.

We had hoped for the best and made a mess by creating the notch babies.

It took a couple of years after the 1977 amendments passed before it became apparent that the economic experience had turned bad. A few Band-Aid devices were used to alleviate the situation somewhat.

The first one was in 1980, when the tax rates for disability insurance and for retirement and survivors insurance got juggled around. This was a bookkeeping transaction that the taxpayer would never see reflected on a pay stub. Part of the taxes that come out of your pay are allocated to the retirement and survivors fund and part go to the disability fund.

As I mentioned earlier, the disability fund was in pretty good shape, so we simply diverted some of that revenue into the retirement and survivors fund to help keep it afloat, while we tried to figure out how to fix the hole in the boat.

It bought us about two years. But, by 1982, it was apparent that the retirement and survivors fund was going to run out of money by the end of the year unless we did something.

That's when we applied the second Band-Aid, allowing the retirement and survivors fund to borrow money from the funds for disability benefits and the hospital benefits part of Medicare. Some $17 billion was borrowed from the two funds combined. The intent of Congress, as stated in committee reports, was that only enough money could be borrowed to keep the fund in the black through the first six months of 1983.

Congress did this very intentionally and acted quite responsibly. In essence it put its own feet to the fire and said: We're not going to give indefinite borrowing authority. We're only going to give enough so that benefits can be paid through the middle of 1983. By the end of 1982, the National Commission on Social Security Reform, which already was being set up at the beginning of that year (to be described in the next chapter), should come out with its report on how to fix the system, and we should then act within six months of that report.

This was the thinking on the Hill. The Administration wasn't sleeping during this time. The problem was talked about before Reagan took the oath of office in 1981. I had served as a member of his transition team, but our role was only to identify what issues the new Administration was going to have to deal with. How to deal with these issues and who should do the dealing wasn't part of our job.

In May 1981, the Administration came out with an eight-point plan. It was under Schweiker's name, so if it got attacked he took the arrows in the chest. This, according to Stockman's account, was done at the insistence of James A. Baker III, who, at the time, was the White House chief of staff. Baker wanted as much distance as he could get between Reagan and this plan. Maybe he knew something that nobody else in the room where the final decision was made could figure out.

Reagan had some intellectual distance here as well. This largely technical, far-reaching plan to overhaul the largest insurance system in the world was presented to him in a one-hour meeting.

We met with Reagan in the White House, and, as this session went on, I happened to look up at the wall where a portrait of Franklin D. Roosevelt was hanging. I couldn't help but think that he had to be spinning in his grave at what they were trying to do to Social Security.

"Only sixty minutes had been allotted for that meeting on May 11 with the President — not much time for him to review a plan which in both philosophy and detail reversed 45 years of Social Security history," Stockman later wrote in his book. "But since only three people in the room ... understood the issues, I assumed that an hour would probably do it.''

Actually, Stockman was wrong in several respects. First, he includes as those who ''understood'' only Schweiker, Marty Anderson, and himself, and, amazingly, not Social Security Commissioner Jack Svahn or myself, who were there to explain the proposal with a chart presentation. Second, the plan did not, by any means, ''reverse 45 years of Social Security history.'' The cuts and rollbacks involved — and such things had happened several times before — were not all that philosophically momentous. If they had been, I would have cashed in my chips, resigned, and gone public on the issues.

The President seemed to be listening very attentively but asked few questions. At the end of the meeting, he expressed general approval of the plan but said that he would have to think more about one alternative which had been presented — covering new federal civilian employees under Social Security. Such a provision was not included in the final proposal (although it was subsequently in the recommendations of the National Commission on Social Security Reform and in the 1983 amendments).

The Administration made the following eight proposals:

(1) Cutting the financial incentives for retiring between the ages of 62 and 65. Under existing law, a worker retiring at age 62 could draw 80 percent of the benefit that would be available by waiting until age 65 to claim the benefits. This is fair — I had devised it in 1956 — because it is neutral as far as the system is concerned. In actuarial terms, a person drawing 80 percent benefits from age 62 until death could expect to get the same grand total (taking into account the time value of money) as drawing 100 percent benefits from age 65 until death. The Administration wanted

to slash this early-retirement figure from 80 percent to 55 percent.

(2) Eliminating "windfall" benefits for workers who drew only the minimum benefit. The theory behind this, which was sound, was that many, if not most, of these workers were already drawing pensions based on non-covered work, probably from governmental employment. They barely qualified to get anything from Social Security, but then got an unduly large benefit compared with what they had contributed. Trying to end this turned into a public relations disaster. (However, something along these lines was done in legislation later in 1981.)

(3) Tightening up requirements to qualify for disability payments. Under the proposed new rules, workers could qualify only for medical reasons (not for a combination of non-medical and medical reasons). They would have to wait six months (instead of five). Their prognosis must show that they would be disabled for at least 24 months (instead of 12 months). And they would have to have been paying taxes into the system for at least 7 1/2 of the last 10 years (instead of five of the last 10 years).

(4) Eliminating benefits for children of early retirees and putting a lower limit on total benefits paid to the family of a worker who has retired or died. In some cases under existing law, the family was drawing almost as much as what the worker had been bringing home in a paycheck.

(5) Taxing all of a worker's sick pay. Previously, the first six months of sick pay had been exempt. (This proposal was enacted in amendments in 1981.)

(6) Ending the earnings test for retirement benefits for persons age 65-69 (as was already done for those age

70 and over). In 1981, a retiree could keep working but could earn only $5,500 a year before Social Security benefits would be cut. The reduction was basically $1 in benefits for every $2 of earnings above the limit. (In 1992, that limit was $10,200, and the reduction was $1 for $3.)

(7) Instituting a small tax cut to take effect in 1985-89, a larger one than that already scheduled under existing law for 1990 through 2019, and a small one thereafter. The 1977 law had set the tax rate at 7.65 percent for 1990 and after. The Administration proposed cutting that to 6.45 percent for 1990 through 2019, and then 7.55 percent after that.

(8) Finally, there were some technical changes, most of which are only worth a mention to say that they were there. The most significant one was to change the month when the annual cost-of-living adjustment is first applicable from June to September. The 1983 amendments actually went further, advancing the COLA date from June to December.

Seven of the eight points proposed by the Reagan Administration were going to save money. The one that was going to cost money was the phasing out of the earnings limit on retirees aged 65-69 who were drawing Social Security. In the first five years, this would have cost the trust fund $6.5 billion.

"The crisis is inescapable," Schweiker said in announcing the Administration's package on May 12, 1981. "It is here. It is now. It is serious. And it must be faced. Today we move to face it head-on and solve it."

The only thing the Reagan Administration faced head-on was the locomotive of public opinion. It would flatten them.

As Deputy Commissioner of Social Security, I had worked on the Administration plan, which actually was a group effort that included people from the Social Security Administration, the Treasury Department, and the Office of Management and Budget. We weren't all there as equals. It was clear from the beginning that the shots were being called by OMB and the Executive Office of the President.

The Administration immediately started catching flak for this plan, and for its support of eliminating the regular minimum benefit in earlier legislative activity. The latter position was rather unfairly criticized because most people thought it was something that it wasn't.

This regular minimum benefit was then (in June 1982) between $122 and $182 a month. It had nothing to do with whether a person was rich or poor, or a low earner or a high earner. It had everything to do with the size of the check that was being written.

This "regular" minimum is not to be confused with the "special" minimum. That's the one that does go to the low earners, generally to people who have been paying into the system for 20 to 30 years. It was intended to provide a decent level of payment to low-income employees such as agricultural workers and domestic workers.

The problem was that many people, some of whom were in Congress, got these two kinds of payments mixed up.

As it was originally conceived in 1935, the regular minimum started out at $10 a month. It was more what might be called a facility of payment. You didn't want to send out checks that were just too small. (Insurance companies do this all the time. If an insurance policy today pays an annuity of less than $25 a month, the company will hang onto the money and pay it quarterly or semi-annually or annually in a more sizeable amount.)

But many people in Congress and elsewhere thought the regular minimum was supposed to take care of low earners, and many people were sympathetic to having a high regular minimum.

So who benefitted by the regular minimum? People who shouldn't have, generally. People like federal government employees who had worked under Civil Service Retirement most of their lives. Then they got a small, part-time job, just barely qualified for Social Security, and received a relatively large benefit. There was really no social need for a large minimum payment in that case.

It was hard to tell what percentage of this group that government employees comprised, but we knew they were there. Social Security didn't have the complete earnings record of everybody — just people who were covered by the system. Government employees didn't show up on radar, unless they landed some part-time job or a job after retiring from the government. Then it looked as though they had skimpy lifetime average earnings, so they got the regular minimum benefit.

But based on analysis and logic, it was known that a lot of these people were government employees who were getting sizeable Civil Service annuities, whether federal, state, or local. There were other people too, such as those who worked only 10 years or so at only nominal part-time wages. They too would get the regular minimum.

There was a great misunderstanding in Congress as to the role of the regular minimum. The knowledgeable people knew that the regular minimum shouldn't, as it was sometimes done in the earlier years, be boosted up much more than general wages increased because of the argument that we've got to take care of the poor people.

The Administration favored the elimination of the regular minimum benefit, not only for all future retirees, but even for people already on the rolls. It would have cut them back considerably in some cases. This proposal actually passed in Congress in 1981 and was signed into law. But it was repealed before the year was out.

I didn't have any trouble with the idea of eliminating this payment for future eligibles, but I did object to taking it away from people who were already getting it. Rightly or wrongly, they were entitled to it legally, and it had become part of their financial planning. You don't just barge in and snatch money out of people's hands.

I told them that. I spoke to my boss, Jack Svahn, and I think he agreed with me. Svahn had worked for the Department of Health, Education, and Welfare and for Reagan out in California in the state's welfare department. Svahn was a nice guy and had a pretty good understanding of how Social Security was supposed to work. But he also knew when he was outgunned, and he wasn't willing to fight the White House on any of this.

Months after this fight was over, Reagan was still defending what he tried to do. His grasp of the facts was certainly creative.

"What I pledged to do was to have a Social Security — to put it on a sound fiscal basis, and yet not at the expense of those people who are presently retired; that you pull the rug out from under them and reduce their benefits," Reagan said in December before a bunch of newspaper editors.

Svahn didn't have to fight this battle. There were 535 people on Capitol Hill who were just itching to do it by the end of the year. At first they rolled over, and in minor, quickie legislation signed into law in 1981, gave Reagan what he wanted, cutting off the regular minimum benefit for those on the rolls, as well as for new eligibles.

This got shoved through Congress because Reagan had that power then. He had a Republican Senate, and he had the Boll Weevils, the conservative Democrats, in the House, giving him a working majority in both houses. Doing away with this minimum payment was tucked into a bigger bill that dealt with larger issues, and it sailed right through.

Then Congress saw what it had done, and there was a firestorm. The issue was reconsidered, and just before the end of the year it was repealed, at least for the people who were already getting the money. Congress really bent over backwards to be fair about this. In addition to the people already drawing the benefit, Congress protected the right of people who were eligible but for one reason or another weren't taking the money. It wouldn't matter when they filed for the benefit but only whether, because of their age, they could have gotten it.

This is a very important principle. The person who reached age 62 in 1981 could get the regular minimum. If he or she didn't apply that year but came in the next year, it was still available. The rationale here was not to take advantage of people's ignorance of what they may have coming to them. If they are eligible for a benefit, they should get it. Social Security legislation was almost always done this way, although it's not always like that anymore because the budgeteers like to pick up some stray cash by taking advantage of those eligibles who are uninformed.

At times in this political process, it seemed that the Social Security Administration was little more than a bystander as its future was being shaped. Our role at these meetings was to give the other people in the room a range of options and to do the calculations to figure out how much someone else's bright idea was going to save the system — or cost it.

Ending the regular minimum benefits is a good case in point. No one who had worked with pensions or knew anything about insurance would dream of ending a benefit for people who are already getting it. But doing this would save the system — and the general budget — $600 million over the first four years. That was all these guys cared about. That was OMB. That was Stockman.

Stockman himself came to some of the meetings. I didn't know him when he was in the Congress. I didn't get to know him very well later, but from what I saw of him at the meetings, he lived up to what was being said about him in the press. Of course I'm colored by what I read. He was a smart guy, there's no question about it. He had a very high opinion of himself.

He was in charge, so OMB decided on what the package ought to be after the discussions of the interdepartmental group. This was a new way of doing business for Social Security. In the past, decisions on how to run the system had always been made within the department. Back in the days when there was a Social Security Board, an independent agency, it made its own recommendations. Even when it became part of the Federal Security Agency, the decisions still came from within.

OMB always had the power to look at these things. The best that can be said is that they hadn't exerted nearly as much influence in the past as they did in this instance. There were at least a couple of reasons for this: Social Security had never been in this much trouble before, and now it was a big political issue.

OMB's role here was a direct outgrowth of Reagan's distrust of the bureaucracy. The White House wanted more control over the government and didn't want the bureaucrats doing it. The Administration thought that the bureaucrats were interested in the system as it was, that they had a built-in bias for the status quo.

The flaw with that argument is that the bureaucrats weren't the guys who loused things up in the first place.

Cutting off the minimum payment wasn't OMB's biggest mistake, though. Without a doubt, that was the bone-headed notion of slashing benefits for people who retire between ages 62 and 65 below the 20 percent actuarially equivalent reduction. For someone planning to retire at 62, the proposed 55 percent factor would have meant a 31 percent cut in benefits compared to what they would have gotten under previous law.

Part of the argument was that the Administration wanted to discourage people from retiring early. I'm in favor of that. But

I think that if you're going to do it, you shouldn't sandbag them. I would have said just don't let people retire at 62, reduction or no reduction, but in practice they do. You can't really treat them unfairly.

The benefits payable for early retirement under present law are actuarially neutral, but I still think early retirement is a bad idea. People should work if they're able. It's good for you.

But Stockman and his crowd weren't looking at building character. The bottom line was that this would have saved some $18 billion between 1982 and 1986.

There was nothing really sacred about retirement at age 62. For the first two decades of Social Security, men could not retire if they were younger than 65. (This was made possible for women in 1956.) Lowering the minimum retirement age to 62 for men was part of an amendment to the law passed in 1961. So we're not talking about some hoary old tradition here. This was a relatively recent notion, and there was nothing wrong with changing it. As long as you did it right.

Nobody knows how long they're going to live. If you knew you were going to die at age 64, you would certainly want to consider retiring and claiming benefits at 62. If you knew you were going to live to 106, you would want to put off retiring for some time after 62. Financially, both of these courses of action would make sense.

The system should make sure that whatever decision an individual makes, the resulting payment is fair — and it usually does so. In technical terms this is called finding the actuarial equivalent. That's why a person retiring at age 62 gets benefits at 80 percent of what would have been collected at age 65. And for retirement between those ages it's on a pro rata basis. It's very fair; there are no sharp edges or notches.

This 80 percent reduction factor isn't pulled out of the air. It's something that comes at the end of a mathematical analysis, which, in fact, I did.

But in 1981 the Administration people went at it backwards. They figured out how much money they wanted to save and worked their way back from that. It came out that their goals would be met if people retiring at age 62 got benefits of only 55 percent of what they would get at 65.

This was more than just a bad way to look at Social Security. It was horrible. It was an outrage!

The 55 percent was just drawn out of the air. They considered how much money would be saved if it was 70 percent or 60 percent or 50 percent. They just came out and said, "Well, 55 percent is as far as we can go." This had nothing to do with actuarial soundness or fairness. It was just a way of saving money. Because roughly half of the people retire at or close to 62, this started saving big sums of money pretty quickly.

I argued very strongly against this but to no avail. I did this at these interdepartmental meetings and all the final meetings. In the entire Social Security Administration, there seemed to be only one person who favored it, and that was Jack Svahn. He was a team player and the President's man.

I had told him at the meetings and in private that this was a bad idea, and I think he agreed. But he said, "Look, they're running the show. We can argue, but they're running the show." What else could he do? He was the commissioner, and he had to be on the team or else.

I didn't come out publicly and say this was a bad idea. It wasn't a big enough issue that I would say, "I'm going public on this. I'm quitting." It wasn't such a big issue that I couldn't stay there and keep working for broader, more important things. I still wanted to be an influence. I'd done my job; I'd said it was a bad idea. I didn't think that they ought to do it. But in the aggregate we had to do something. And there were things in this 1981 package that were very good.

In hindsight you can be awfully smart. As time went by I came to realize more and more how bad this 55 percent proposal was. I didn't realize the full extent of its weakness at the time. And nobody else did either. The political fallout aside, this was just bad policy.

But the Senate, controlled 53-47 by the Republicans, picked up on the politics quickly. They knew this idea was death. So barely a week had gone by since Schweiker rolled the proposal out in front of the public, and already it was causing debate on the Senate floor.

Sen. Bob Dole, chairman of the Finance Committee, introduced a committee resolution saying that "Congress shall not precipitously and unfairly penalize early retirees."

It passed 96-0.

The Democrats earlier had put up a much stronger resolution saying that what the Administration was doing was "a breach of faith" with the nation's elderly. That failed by just one vote — and three Republicans had abstained. Dole, a Republican from Kansas, got the more-mildly worded resolution through. But even Dole didn't mince words when it came to the President's proposal. "Some things he suggests have great merit," Dole said in a speech on the Senate floor. "Some have less, and a few have little."

The Administration got the message and immediately signalled that it was willing to compromise, but it didn't withdraw the "Schweiker" proposal, at least not for a few ugly months.

So the gears of Congress continued to grind. This proposal, although largely considered to be dead on arrival, nevertheless was sent through the mill of hearings as though someone seriously thought it had a chance. The Ways and Means Committee in the House and the Finance Committee in the Senate put it on their calendars.

Besides, everyone knew we had to do something about Social Security, but no one could agree on what that ought to be. Time was running out.

So I had to go to the Hill and explain the rationale behind this proposal, including the parts that I deeply disliked. I was a good soldier. I had had somewhat the same thing occur back in 1956 when I was Chief Actuary of the Social Security Administration.

At that time Congress was holding hearings on including monthly disability benefits in the program, and the Eisenhower Administration hadn't made up its mind on the matter because there was a lot of opposition. Business and the insurance companies didn't want it, and some of the Republicans didn't want disability benefits because they said you couldn't administer it through the government. So the Administration asked me to go up and testify as Chief Actuary, to explain factually what was in the bill. I was not to advocate it, but just to explain it and discuss its financing aspects.

It was not quite the same set of circumstances in 1981 as it was in 1956. This time I was a little more of an advocate. I explained why the Administration favored the bill and favored each provision. I said that I was there to give the Administration's position, not my views, and that when I gave facts and figures, I stood fully in back of them. Still, I was a little queasy about what I was doing.

One reason was a discovery that we'd made back in the office in the weeks since the proposal was unveiled. My actuarial assistant, Bruce Schobel, and I had figured this out, and we were horrified.

This was the dirty little secret: the 55 percent proposal wasn't just unfair, but it was especially cruel to low- and middle-income people.

Balancing the system on the backs of the poor and the middle class was the very thing that the Administration had long been accused of doing. Of course, everyone from the President on down denied this.

But here it was. I don't know that the Administration did it on purpose. Maybe if they'd really been trying to protect the interests of the poor and middle class, this wouldn't have happened. But it got through and was in the proposal, and I was praying that nobody but Bruce and I had caught it.

Here is how this inequity worked. Suppose you're age 62. You don't have a job anymore. You've either been forced to retire, or you just felt you had to retire because of health. You, in essence, would be forced to take the early-retirement benefit in order to have something to live on, even though it was a bad deal.

However, the high-paid guy in the same situation who retired at age 62, either voluntarily or involuntarily, can afford to wait until age 65 and take the unreduced benefit. Furthermore, he or she can have the private pension that's beginning at age 62 reallocated on an actuarially equivalent basis, in essence front-loaded, so they get a larger benefit between ages 62 and 65 and have it scaled back when the full Social Security benefit kicks in at age 65.

Private pension plans can easily do that. There's nothing illegal or unethical about it. Actuarially they can do it so that it doesn't cost the plan anything. So the high-paid guy with the pension, or even the moderately high-paid, could avoid the whole inequity that the proposal would create.

This situation, if discovered and publicized, would have been a political nightmare for the Reagan Administration. There was no question but that the little guy would take it in the neck, and the richer would not get hurt. This situation would have played right into the hands of the Democrats, but they didn't know they had this weapon. No one thought to ask me about it in the congressional hearings or elsewhere, so I didn't bring it up. Besides, the success of the Dole resolution, passed overwhelmingly in May, made it clear that the 55 percent proposal was dead anyway.

I knew the thing was so bad it was going to be killed anyway, so I testified at the hearings. The committee members were kind to me. They listened to what I had to say. Some of them said that this was a terrible plan, but they didn't blame me for it, even though they knew I had worked on it.

The criticism was universal. Very few Republicans did anything other than criticize it. Two weeks to the day after I testified before Pickle's subcommittee, the Reagan Administration caved in.

Baker and presidential counselor Edwin Meese did a report card on the Reagan Administration's first year in office. As they surveyed the wreckage of Social Security, they bravely gave their boss the grade which they thought he deserved: an A-plus. The White House is probably the only place outside of George Orwell Elementary School where somebody can louse up that badly and still claim a place on the honor roll.

Baker and Meese said they were giving Reagan a high grade for his "political courage and effort."

Later, in his autobiography *An American Life* [13], Reagan lamented the disintegration of his grand plan to fix Social Security once and for all:

> "We had to withdraw a plan to cut billions of dollars in waste and fraud from the Social Security system — among other abuses, we'd discovered monthly Social Security checks were being sent to eighty-five hundred people who'd been dead an average of 81 months — after the Democrats began accusing us of plotting to throw senior citizens to the wolves."

Oh, please. That's just fiction. I'll admit that it sometimes takes the system a while to sort out the dead from the living, but much of that money is eventually recovered, and besides that's not the reason the system was in trouble. Nobody can argue with cutting out waste and fraud, but what Stockman and his people tried to commit was a fraud in itself. Thank goodness lots of people were able to see through it.

So on September 24, 1981, Reagan went on television and addressed the nation from the Oval Office. He blamed the Democratic majority in the House for stalling on Social Security reform.

There was some truth to that. Jake Pickle had been ready to go full tilt to find a solution to Social Security's problems, but House Speaker Tip O'Neill told him to stop. Next year would be an election year, and this was going to be a political issue, O'Neill told him. Let the Republicans worry about it.

Nine months had gone by, and we were no closer to repairing Social Security than we were on the day Reagan took office. The White House was feeling the heat, and the system was heading for collapse. Reagan announced that he was setting up a 15-member commission to deal with the problem. He would appoint five members, Senate Republican leader Howard Baker would appoint five, and O'Neill would appoint five on behalf of the House. The composition of the commission and its assignment was worked out well in advance with congressional leaders from both parties.

The President said this task force would "review all the options and come up with a plan that assures the fiscal integrity of Social Security and that Social Security recipients will continue to receive their full benefits."

It's an old saying that a committee is a group of the unwilling, chosen from the unfit to do the unnecessary. But it was plain to me right away that this commission was going to be none of that. This panel, which would be known as the National Commission on Social Security Reform, was going to recommend more basic changes in Social Security than at any time since the system was invented.

The system was going to be reformed from the outside, not from within, and I wanted to be where the work was going to be done. To do that I'd have to leave the Social Security Administration again.

It was love, not money, that had brought me back to work for the Social Security Administration in 1981 after an almost 11-year absence.   Because of provisions in federal law against "double dippers" drawing both a fat Civil Service Retirement pension and a government paycheck, I all but lost money on the deal. After taking into account my $50,112 annual Civil Service Retirement pension, my initial pay for being Deputy Commissioner of Social Security came to $3,224 a year.   That worked out to $1.55 an hour, assuming I only worked a 40-hour week.

So I wasn't leaving a lot behind when I decided to quit. I hoped that, on the outside, given my years of experience I would be a logical choice for appointment to the new commission. At least it seemed logical to me. I had lobbied for it on the Hill, but didn't get any firm commitments.

On my way out, I wanted to take one last swipe at Stockman, who at times had condemned Social Security as a "Ponzi scheme" and "closet Socialism."

I just thought that this was my one chance to say what needed to be said. I'd been a good soldier up to this point, and I just thought that these people at OMB should keep their dirty little hands off Social Security and not use it as a tool for their political, economic or budgetary purposes.

So on December 14, 1981 I sent my letter of resignation to Secretary Schweiker, which read as follows:

———

Dear Mr. Secretary:

I am submitting my resignation as Deputy Commissioner of Social Security for Programs, effective January 8, 1982.   The reason for this action is that, with only the moderate and very short-range solutions to the financing problems of the Social Security system which have been enacted, I foresee that the necessary more permanent, long-range legislative action will not occur for several years.

I have been very honored and pleased to serve under your leadership in the past months in connection with the vital matter of restructuring the Social Security program so as to put it on a sound financial basis. I strongly support the general principles that the Administration has advocated in this connection, and also the vast majority of the specific proposals that have been made to do this. It is truly unfortunate that only a small portion of these proposals has been enacted into law, and that the real problem is yet to be faced.

Although I continue to support fully the Administration's position in this area, I am constrained to say that the legislative development procedures in the Executive Branch do not seem to me to be nearly as effective as they might be. Specifically, I am referring to the many layers of clearance and review — not only as to major political issues, but also as to minor policy and technical points at levels above the Social Security Administration. This occurs both in the Department and in higher organizations, such as the Office of Management and Budget.

In particular, the latter agency (and especially its civil service employees) develops policy without regard to the social and economic aspects of the Social Security program — and even the political aspects. This was well exemplified by the disastrous results that occurred from the proposal to eliminate the minimum benefit for all persons currently on the rolls and also from the proposal to sharply increase the early-retirement reduction factor.

In conclusion, Mr. Secretary, I want to express my great appreciation for the opportunity to serve you and the Reagan Administration in connection with this very important problem. I only hope that I have made at least some contribution to its resolution.

Sincerely yours,

Within a week it hit the papers. ''Republican Social Security Expert Quits in Anger'' was the headline in *The Washington Post.*

Schweiker and Svahn, nevertheless, were gracious. ''In the year that you have served us, we have benefited much from your great experience and wise counsel,'' Secretary Schweiker wrote to me in reply. ''I know that you remain as deeply committed as ever to the Social Security program.''

Commissioner Svahn's statement was equally kind: ''He has been with Social Security from its beginning, and his formal departure from Social Security will by no means lessen his intense devotion to the program that he has done so much to build.'' Svahn was unhappy about my leaving and wanted me to stick around. I could have been a lot of help to him because it was obvious that Social Security was in for big changes, and my background and experience could have come in pretty handy.

But Svahn, the Reagan loyalist, was pleased with the way I chose to go out. He didn't like what Stockman was doing any more than I did, so on top of his kind words for me when I left, Svahn gave me a placque with a Commissioner's Citation, which I've still got hanging on my wall.

So now I was back on the outside again, hoping to get back in. I didn't have to wait long for the verdict. Two days after my letter to Schweiker, Reagan announced the membership of the commission. There were eight Republicans and seven Democrats.

The following were appointed by the President: Robert A. Beck, chief executive officer of Prudential Insurance Company of

America; Mary Falvey Fuller, vice president for finance of Shaklee Corp.; Alan Greenspan, then a member of the President's economic policy advisory board and chairman of Townsend-Greenspan and Co. (and now chairman of the Federal Reserve Board); Alexander B. Trowbridge, president of the National Association of Manufacturers; and Joe D. Waggonner, Jr., a former Louisiana congressman and now a bank consultant. The latter two were Democrats.

The Senate appointed Sen. William Armstrong, R-Colo., Sen. Robert Dole, R-Kan., Sen. John Heinz, R-Pa., Sen. Daniel Patrick Moynihan, D-N.Y., and AFL-CIO President Lane Kirkland.

The House appointed Rep. Claude D. Pepper, D-Fla., Rep. William Archer, R-Texas, Rep. Barber Conable, R-N.Y., former Social Security Commissioner Robert M. Ball, and former Rep. Martha Keys, D-Kan.

My hope had been to be a Senate Republican appointee, since I was liked and respected there. But I had a real handicap — I wasn't a senator. I didn't make the commission. Now I was really out! Out of the government and out of the action entirely.

CHAPTER TWO

AT THE LAST POSSIBLE MINUTE

This was the second time in my life that I had reached for the brass ring and came up with a handful of air. The first time was about a dozen years earlier when I wanted to be Commissioner of Social Security and didn't get it.

But even though I wasn't appointed to the new commission to reform the program, I wasn't giving up on the idea yet. When President Reagan signed his executive order setting up the commission on December 16, 1981, there was this passage near the end of the document: "The commission shall have a staff headed by an executive director."

It was, in other words, to have its own tiny bureaucracy. This wasn't exactly what I had wanted, but it certainly beat the alternative, which was sitting around my house reading about all this in the papers. I had been present at Social Security's birth, and I wanted to be there for its rebirth. So what if I was a bureaucrat instead of an elder statesman? I'd been a bureaucrat all my life and found it to be an honorable profession.

I went back to my sponsors on Capitol Hill and said that I wanted to be considered for the job. Again, I didn't get a strong commitment.   After all, they weren't doing the hiring.   The appointment had to come from President Reagan.

Sen. Dole didn't commit himself.   "Well, that's a good idea," he said.   "We'll see what can be done."

There had to have been some talking going on behind the scenes, because to the best of my recollection, I didn't discuss this job with anybody in the Reagan Administration.   So the only way they could have found out I was interested was when Dole told them.

I'd been in government for nearly a half century, and I still considered myself lousy at playing politics.   At least I didn't like it very much.   I didn't have the stomach to do the lobbying that it took to get to the top, and I didn't have the gamesman's instinct to want to find out who was doing what to whom — or more importantly, who was doing what to me.

But I didn't feel too uncomfortable talking to Dole or the Republicans in the House.   I had worked with these people for years and knew them well.   They came through for me.

I was told some time later that the reason I got the job wasn't just that the Republicans in Congress liked me, but also the Democrats found me acceptable.   That doesn't mean they were ready to run up and throw their arms around me.   It's sort of like the advice and consent which the Senate gives for presidential appointees.   A vote for a guy just means they don't find him objectionable, or at least he is more acceptable than some others might be.

When my appointment was finally announced in late December 1981, I was in Bermuda doing some annual work that I do for that government's hospital insurance system.   The one person who tracked me down to congratulate me was Sen. Pat Moynihan, a Democrat.

On the same day that Reagan signed the executive order establishing the commission, he also announced the appointment of its members and that Alan Greenspan would be serving as the chairman. So at some point after my conversation with Dole, I got a call from the White House telling me to meet with the newly appointed chairman for an interview.

All I knew of Greenspan up to that point was what I'd read about him in the papers. He had been in the news quite a bit over the years, having advised presidents on the state of the economy, which was usually in trouble, which was why the presidents were asking him what to do. Although he had no special knowledge of Social Security, he was well suited to this new task. He'd had a lot of experience dealing with big financial problems.

So on the appointed day, I went down to the White House, and once I got through security, I was escorted to the Old Executive Office Building to meet Greenspan. We didn't say a lot, and the meeting was really pretty brief. He evidently had some background on who I was and what I'd done. This was sort of the final step in the process of hiring me. As chairman he had every right to say who would be in charge of the store when he wasn't there. We talked for a while, we got along fine, we shook hands, and I left.

I don't know just who told me that I had been appointed Executive Director. I do recall that the call came from the White House, asking me to come over and take my oath of office. It was pretty much of a *pro forma* thing. There was no ceremony. It was purely a clerical procedure. I don't remember anything about it except that I had to sign a stack of personnel forms. Greenspan wasn't there. It was sort of like getting a driver's license.

Once I got the job, they arranged for temporary office space for me in the Old Executive Office Building. I was there for a week or two. Greenspan didn't have an office. He flew in from New York when he needed to come to Washington and left when his business was done.

For our "permanent" offices (as permanent as a temporary commission can be), we were being quartered in one of the choicest pieces of real estate in Washington: a townhouse on

Jackson Square, across the street from the White House. The house we were getting, down toward the end of the block, had once been occupied by President Theodore Roosevelt as a temporary White House when repairs were being made on the real one.

I obviously didn't pick the house. The White House assigned it to us and said, "We hope you like it." The location itself carried a message. The White House wanted to show that it held the work of the commission in high regard.

It was really a neat place, high ceilings, cornices, marble fireplaces, and crystal chandeliers. There was no elevator, so we had to walk up three floors. My office was on the second floor, with a view of Lafayette Square and the White House, and my parking spot was right out front. I had two of the most coveted perks in Washington — a great view and a parking place.

Greenspan's office, for the times he was there, was on the third floor. The first floor was sort of a reception area and conference rooms. The other commissioners didn't have offices.

The Social Security Administration was essentially going to be the administrative manager of the operation. They were to assign someone to me to be the administrative officer.

The staff of the commission was only about 10 people. Some would come and go over the course of our mission, and some others would work there only part-time. Our first task was to get the place set up, get some furniture, and hire some people.

Right away the congressional Democratic members of the commission lined up three people whom they wanted hired. They all had good professional qualifications, but I wasn't completely enthusiastic about having them on the staff. And the Democrats wanted all of them hired at top dollar, which at the time was $57,500.

I wrote Greenspan a note, saying it was okay with me to hire Merton Bernstein, a law professor at Washington University in St. Louis, Elizabeth Duskin, the research director for the

National Council of Senior Citizens (an AFL-CIO sponsored group), and Eric Kingson, a professor of social work at the University of Maryland. All three were hired, and we got along fine.

At the suggestion of Chairman Greenspan, I also hired Nancy Altman, a former aide to Sen. John Danforth, R-Mo., and Carolyn Weaver, an economist who was working on Dole's staff and is now at the American Enterprise Institute, a conservative think tank in Washington.

Through the kindness of Jack Svahn, I was able to "borrow" on a full-time basis three people who had been on my personal staff when I was Deputy Commissioner — Bruce Schobel (an actuary), Suzanne Dilk, and Annette Coates. Several other top-notch Social Security Administration staff members were loaned on a part-time basis. I really had a great staff.

Oh, yes, I was being paid too. Nominally, it was $63,800, but because I was already drawing a government pension, the net salary was going to work out to about $10,566 a year.

The White House didn't chip in anybody and may have been trying to keep some political distance. Stockman, the author of last year's disaster, was still around, but if he was trying to influence the commission, I didn't see it. Of course, you could make the case that the White House had all the influence it wanted. Greenspan, after all, had been appointed by the President. But Greenspan is somebody who knows his own mind, and while he has advised the last few presidents, he nevertheless is able to maintain his intellectual independence.

He is sort of an introspective guy, and later in the process, when it looked as though everything was falling apart, he talked freely with me. He wasn't really chatty, but he did tell me what I needed to know, and I was quite content with our relationship.

On February 27, 1982, the commission met for the first time. It was at first planned to be a no-frills affair in the New Executive Office Building, and we were going to have lunch brought in. We ended up moving it to a hotel because it was cheaper. For some later meetings, we'd get free space on the Hill, courtesy of the Congress.

About 100 people showed up at the Sheraton-Carlton Hotel to watch that morning, as Greenspan gaveled the commission to order.

Item One was a letter from President Reagan. "The nation will be watching with great interest the work and progress of the National Commission on Social Security Reform," the President wrote to the commission. "On behalf of all Americans, I wish you success as you begin your deliberations."

Fourteen of the fifteen members were there, with Sen. Armstrong being the only one who couldn't make it. Although I wouldn't read anything into his absence, Armstrong didn't seem to like the idea of this commission, didn't like the mix of people appointed to it and didn't even like being a member of it himself. Just a month earlier, he had told a meeting of the American Association of Retired Persons and the National Retired Teachers Association that he thought the commission would probably wind up producing only another report on the problem that would do little more than collect dust somewhere. That truly was one of the dangers, and he was awfully close to being right.

The first meeting was mostly procedural. Commission members decided that they wouldn't divide up into subcommittees or set up an executive committee. This was an idea that in a way had to be junked later on, when the commission was paralyzed by division.

They also decided — wisely so — not to hold public hearings. The meetings were going to be open, but they weren't going to be taking any testimony. They didn't need to. This subject already had been talked nearly to death. Literally!

Counting is something that I do well. So on the day before this first meeting, I sent Greenspan a note that gave some kind of measure of how much hot air had been let loose in the name of

Social Security since the beginning of 1979, when it was generally recognized that we were heading for collapse. I looked over the records of an advisory council, one study group, two presidential commissions, and the work of a number of congressional committees. There had been a total of 211 hearings, where 2,539 witnesses had testified.

That was enough. There wasn't anything that could be said that hadn't been said already. Listening to witnesses would be an unnecessary distraction and waste valuable time that we just didn't have. The time had come to cut through all of this and make some decisions.

Once the commissioners figured out how they were going to operate, they had to be brought up to speed on just what they were working on. These were people of varying backgrounds, divergent ideologies, and differing levels of knowledge of the Social Security system. Of course, people like Bob Ball knew a great deal about the system. Some of the members of Congress had worked on the subject for years and were reasonably knowledgeable. There were others in this category, too. For example, Bob Beck, who was CEO of The Prudential Life Insurance Company, had a great knowledge of insurance, of course, and some knowledge of Social Security. The same was true of Alexander Trowbridge of the National Association of Manufacturers. Kirkland too had some knowledge.

So the rest of this first meeting was sort of like a seminar with charts and graphs and some memos. But it was mostly oral presentations. I gave a history of Social Security from its inception to date, speaking all the while from first-hand knowledge. (This led Greenspan to remark, "Of course we don't need a library because we have Bob Myers.")

I also described what the cost estimates showed, what type of cost estimates there were that went out 75 years, and why they went out 75 years. I spent some time on why it was important to look not just at next year because this was a long-range social insurance program. I also laid out the nature of the problem.

I made it clear that the further out in the future we would project, the softer the numbers become. It's just like the pattern fired by a shotgun: the farther away from the barrel you get, the more spread out the pellets are. So projecting costs 75 years in the future means that you'll get a range, sometimes a wide range, and our best guess lies somewhere between the two extremes.

But predicting the near future can be pretty precise. Under almost any conceivable conditions, we knew that we were going to go over the cliff around the middle of 1983 and that nothing would prevent it other than significant legislative changes.

The staff got together and presented various options about what could be done to solve the problem, both in the short run and the long run. And these were a complete range of options — from doing it completely by raising taxes, doing it entirely by cutting benefits, having different kinds of benefit cuts, extending coverage to new groups, or instituting income taxation of benefits.

We tried to cover all the possibilities. Now, it could be argued that if we had limited the options presented to the commission, we could have influenced the outcome. I'll admit that doing something like that is certainly possible. We just didn't.

Of course, we couldn't think of everything, but we could get close to it. This is the way that things worked at the Office of the Actuary at the Social Security Administration. Over the years all sorts of proposals were made by different people for changing benefits — increasing them, decreasing them, and creating new ones. We developed a book of tables, showing various changes in benefits and what their cost effects would be on the system.

Suppose you lower the normal retirement age (at which unreduced benefits are first available) from 65 to 60, or you raise the retirement age to 66, 67, or 68. It was sort of like a cookbook. This is done for the long-range costs, showing the effect over 75 years.

Greenspan right away seemed interested in the idea of raising the retirement age, which had been set at 65 since the system started paying out benefits in 1940. The world obviously had changed since 1940, and among other things, people were now living longer. Given this increase in life expectancy, Greenspan wanted to know what age today is roughly equivalent to age 65 before World War II. I wrote back that the age was 71 (actually 73 for women and 69 for men). In other words, a 71-year-old person could expect to live past that age by the same number of years as a 65-year-old individual could have in 1940.

I didn't suggest raising the retirement age to 71, but I did give some figures on raising it to 68 by the turn of the century. You can't do things like this too quickly. For equity and humaneness, they have to be phased in. So assuming that 65 was the "proper" retirement age in 1982, with rising life expectancies the "proper" retirement age two decades hence would be 68.

One thing we wanted to keep the commission out of, though, was Medicare. Time was short, and Medicare was a separate, although related, issue. I wrote Greenspan that discussion should be strictly limited to the problems of Social Security's Old-Age, Survivors, and Disability Insurance Trust Funds.

"Undoubtedly, there will be pressure to go beyond this," I wrote to the chairman. Greenspan was able to withstand this pressure, and Medicare stayed off to the side.

To say that the commission was politically diverse was not to do it justice. On the one hand, it was fair because everybody was represented. It included ultra-conservatives like Armstrong and ultra-liberals like Claude Pepper. For that reason, some people believed that it was doomed from the very beginning to be paralyzed.

It was a major triumph just to convince some of these people that there really was a problem with Social Security in the first place. Pepper, for example, was a knowledgeable man who paid a great deal of attention to this subject. But he was sure that the alleged ills and problems of the Social Security system were a plot by the Reaganites, who were trying to destroy the program. As I've already pointed out, the Reagan people did try to water down the program, but they didn't have to look for an excuse. It was there, and it was very real.

Other members of the commission recognized that the internal problem was going to be the vast political differences represented there. Ball suggested that we mix up the seating arrangement for the meetings by drawing names out of a hat, so that people would wind up sitting next to someone different every time. That was fine, but this was a much more profound problem than could be solved merely by playing musical chairs.

Anyway, it didn't work. By May 1982, when we held our third meeting, at times the members were calling each other names and once nearly sank into an uncontrollable shouting match. However, Greenspan was a genius at "pouring oil on the troubled waters," and he kept meetings going on a more or less even keel.

Heinz, a moderate Republican, had proposed removing Social Security from the federal budget because he was tired of hearing that his party was trying to balance the budget on the backs of the system's beneficiaries.

Social Security actually has very little to do with the general federal budget. The system by law is self-supporting; it collects its own taxes, and it pays its own benefits and administrative expenses. But because of its nature, it occasionally runs up what some call annual surpluses (actually excesses of income over outgo), socking money away during years of plenty to cover later years when expenses are projected to be higher. This money is invested in government bonds, which pay interest into Social Security's trust funds.

For much of its history, Social Security was recognized as the peculiar budgetary creature it was, and so its funds were not counted as part of the federal financial picture.

Then came Lyndon Johnson and the Vietnam War. The President needed something to mask the deficits which the government was running up to pay for the war, so he started counting Social Security's surplus funds as part of the federal kitty. In government-speak, this was called a "unified budget." In reality it was a sham. The government lacks the authority to spend this money on anything but Social Security, and Social Security lacks the authority to get its money from anywhere else. So putting it in the budget gives people the mistaken impression that the government has money, say, for putting a new wing on the local veterans hospital or buying some park land.

It's a bookkeeping trick that makes the deficit seem artificially lower. Whether you like this generally depends on whether or not you're the President.

Democrats and moderate Republicans were in favor of taking Social Security out of the budget, and Heinz was doing this even though his own party was in the White House and, at least for the moment, was benefitting from LBJ's legacy.

Moynihan was impatient and didn't mind saying so. He didn't have any quarrel with Heinz's proposal, but it was a side issue. Social Security was going broke fast. And this wasn't going to do anything to solve the problem.

Moynihan reminded the commission that the Senate Budget Committee had demanded that Social Security's annual spending be cut by $40 billion, and Pepper reminded his colleagues that the President had said that benefits would not be cut. He wanted to know how that was to be done. How could they cut spending without touching Social Security's main expense, benefits?

"This commission has been compromised," Pepper said.

Moynihan then launched into a general attack on the Reagan Administration. That rankled Armstrong, who accused Moynihan of being a demagogue.

Pepper told Greenspan to tell Armstrong to shut up.

And so it went.

It had become quickly obvious that there was a good likelihood that this commission wasn't going to be able to produce anything. In fact, even at the first meeting, Greenspan joked about it, saying that the commission might wind up so fragmented that at the end of its mission it would issue 15 separate reports on what to do because the members wouldn't be able to agree.

This kind of bickering dragged on through the spring and the summer. By late August, we were trying to sort out the competing proposals, and there were separate meetings between commission members to see if there was some way of brokering an agreement. As individuals, their opinions were all over the place.

Overall, though, the members did tend to gravitate into two camps — basically the five congressionally appointed Democratic liberals on one side, and the five congressionally appointed Republicans and the three Republicans and the two conservative Democrats appointed by President Reagan on the other side.

On August 23 I sent a note to Greenspan outlining as best I could what these two groups stood for and what they wanted. There were some secondary areas of agreement. For example, both sides generally favored bringing federal government employees into the Social Security system along with a supplementary pension plan (as is done for employees in private industry), instead of having the Civil Service Retirement program maintained separately for them. The two sides also agreed that employees of charitable, educational, and religious non-profit organizations should be covered compulsorily (instead of the voluntary basis then applicable), and that state and local governments who had elected coverage in the past could not pull out of the program in the future.

But on the big issues, they were as far apart as ever. On changing the retirement age, the conservatives wanted to raise it from 65 to 68 between the years 2001 and 2012. The liberals didn't want any part of that. On financing, the conservatives favored relatively modest tax rate increases, which then could be reduced once the system was judged to be financially sound. The liberals wanted a steeper increase in the Social Security tax rate that would be offset by an income tax credit. Essentially the effect on the taxpayer would be neutral. The money to float Social Security, in the form of income tax credits, was going to be coming out of the government's general fund, which already was running in the red (and in fact was borrowing money from Social Security).

This impasse remained on into the fall, and we kept hoping that somehow things would work themselves out. Maybe the pressure of the approaching deadlines or the clamor of public opinion would whip the commission into reaching an agreement. Such a thing is certainly not unusual. Congress often finds itself in late-night sessions trying to agree on legislation to let the government keep spending money. Occasionally, under such circumstances, the government has to "shut down," and a few national shrines get padlocked for a day or so. It never lasts long, and chasms that seemed too wide to bridge just a week ago suddenly were not so broad or deep.

Dole was hopeful that some kind of agreement would be reached late in the year, sometime after the election, and he wanted Congress to be ready to act on it. On September 1 he sent a letter to the President, the Speaker of the House and the Senate Majority Leader, calling for convening a special session of Congress after the election to deal with the Social Security problem before the year was out.

"Short of some major change in the composition of the House or Senate, a post-election session would seem most appropriate," Dole wrote. "As I see it, there is a real window of opportunity for positive action after the election and before the

98th Congress convenes. Political pressures would be at a minimum. We would be free of other legislative responsibilities and able to concentrate exclusively on Social Security.''

He said that the special session would save time, because the nation wouldn't have to wait for a new Congress to get organized, and some of the pressure that would be on the next Congress to cut the budget wouldn't be there yet.

"Social Security must be resolved prior to this time; otherwise, the charge will be made that Social Security is being manipulated to balance the federal budget," Dole further wrote. "Those who wish to use the issue for partisan political purposes may prey upon the fears of the elderly and render responsible action impossible.''

There already were groups out there doing exactly what Dole was worried about. Perhaps the most notorious was the organization headed by Jimmy Roosevelt, FDR's son. It was making a pretty good living by using direct mail to scare the daylights out of people and asking them to send in money to help ''save'' Social Security.

Dole concluded, ''When the National Commission reports its recommendations for Social Security reform to Congress, we should be prepared to move quickly.'' He was caught up in the same wishful thinking as the rest of us.

The November meeting was supposed to be the last one. By presidential order the commission was to go out of business on New Year's Eve, so assuming that everything came together at this meeting, there would be enough time to write the report and close down the operation.

The meetings, of course, were entirely open, but there was a lot of backroom negotiating going on as the commission tried to reach a consensus. There were packages put up by both the conservatives and the liberals that would do the job financially. Actuarially they were sound, but they differed in their approaches, one side wanting primarily to cut benefits and the other wanting primarily to raise taxes. So the two sides could not come anywhere near to an agreement.

The congressionally appointed Democrats wanted to do most of the package by raising taxes and the other members, the majority of the commission, wanted to do it by reducing benefits. The commission knew this process wasn't like getting legislation through Congress, where it doesn't matter if a bill passes by one vote or by 300 votes. For the commission, if it recommended something by a split vote of 8-7, or 9-6, or 10-5, that wasn't enough, especially since the House was controlled by Democrats.

The conservatives had a working majority of 10 to 5 on the commission, meaning that they had to swing two or three of the liberal votes to make any package salable on Capitol Hill. Given this problem, I think that Greenspan handled things extremely well. He didn't take formal votes because he didn't want positions to be set in concrete. People had to have the freedom to change their minds without appearing to do so. Some of these people, after all, were politicians who were going to have to explain themselves to fellow members of Congress when the legislation would be considered and also to the voters.

Informally, it was understood that anything the commission did had to be unanimous or nearly so. Everybody recognized that it had to be that way, or else it wasn't going to sail through Congress. We had hoped that, by the November meeting, we would reach consensus.

Even as the meeting opened in a hotel in the historic district of Alexandria, Va. during November 11-13, there still seemed to be time to pull something together. This session was to last three days, and about 400 people showed up each day to watch. I was as curious about what was going to happen as they were.

The commission, in front of these 400 people, in front of the President, the Congress, and the nation, was about to do a swan dive into an empty swimming pool.

The agreement which we all hoped for just didn't show up. The members talked all around the problem, and nobody gave an inch. This passage from the minutes is eloquent testimony to the kinds of things on which they were able to concur:

"The National Commission also tentatively agreed to commend the Social Security Administration on a recent decision that all new and replacement Social Security cards would be printed on banknote paper."

Big deal! If that isn't rearranging the deck chairs on the Titanic, I don't know what is. This was worse than humiliating. We had let the country down. I felt sick.

When we adjourned at the end of the third day, the situation didn't have an air of finality to it. The commission planned to keep working on the problem and to see if it couldn't pull something together in December.

A month later, on December 10, we were in a hearing room in the Dirksen Senate Office Building for another "final" meeting. The only thing that anyone had to say was that there was nothing to say. More black smoke from the chimney.

There was deep gloom in the winter air. The fact still remained that somebody had to do something, and Congress would have to do something. Otherwise, come the middle of 1983, the fund balance would be down to zero, and the checks weren't going to go out on time. Thirty-six million people were looking for that government envelope in their mail at the first of every month.

There wasn't going to be anything gradual about this. Social Security had to have the money to send out all of the checks, or it couldn't send out any of them. You can't say that we'll send them out for Maine, New Hampshire, and Vermont.

We now had less than two weeks to do what we couldn't do in two years. In the meantime, the commission was going out of business in three weeks, it had to produce a report, and there was nothing to write about.

The press had plenty to write about, though, and we were taking our lumps. Donald J. Lambro, a conservative syndicated columnist, delivered this swift kick in the pants in early 1983 [1]:

MOST COWARDLY — The 15-member, blue-ribbon National Commission on Social Security Reform was entrusted with the job of recommending ways to avert the impending bankruptcy of the $175 billion Social Security program. But its members were incapable, or unwilling, to come up with the needed solutions by the December 31, 1982 deadline.

As this issue goes to press, a two-week extension has been granted, and they may yet come through for the 36 million people who depend on Social Security's benefits. Yet the failure of this bipartisan panel to come forth with a workable compromise solution must rank as one of the biggest disappointments of 1982. They knew their duty but refused to fulfill it.

The White House still hoped some progress could be made, so on December 23, the President signed a one-sentence executive order, extending the commission's life to January 15.

As the 98th Congress convened in early January, Dole and Moynihan struck up a chat on the Senate floor. This isn't something you'll find in the Congressional Record. Often when there's a vote, or a quorum call, or even while someone else is standing up giving an impassioned speech, you can see the senators here and there around the Senate chamber talking to each other.

Dole and Moynihan were having one of those conversations, and they quickly decided that this was worth another try. But the commission just wasn't working, and they wanted the freedom to work in private. So this was going to be a different group, one that chose its own membership and one that met in secrecy.

The next day Moynihan met with Dole in his office, and I was there to provide advice. (This was recorded much later, in the Congressional Record for April 7, 1992.)

The two of them, of course, were members of the group; so were Ball, Stockman, Greenspan, and Conable. Jim Baker, the President's chief of staff, and Richard Darman, a presidential assistant, also attended. There were Democrats and Republicans, and there was the Hill and the White House. Not all of this group were members of the commission, so its secret meetings didn't break the law that said all meetings of the commission had to be in public.

It was this group that eventually forged the agreement that saved the system. Much has been made of its membership and the secrecy in which it operated. Political scientist Paul Light called them the "Gang of Nine" in his book *Artful Work: The Politics of Social Security Reform* [10].

In the first place, it wasn't nine, and in the second place, it wasn't a gang. That's just a cute way to write. Too bad it wasn't so. The fact is that people came and went, so the number of participants kept changing. There was nothing sinister about what they were doing. They were trying to save Social Security. That was good.

Although he was a Congressional Fellow in Conable's office, Light was far from the center of the action here. He says that his account is based in part on interviews with sources whose identities he cannot reveal. That's all well and good. The problem is that some of these anonymous sources apparently didn't know what they were talking about. I read the book and found errors and glaring omissions. I counted them (of course), and there were 71 in all. I take the space here to talk about someone else's book simply because I think that I owe a debt to history. It should be told straight.

Light wasn't in the room while these talks were going on, and, sadly, neither was I.

I wanted to be there, but I couldn't be. Nobody ever gave me a good reason why, although there were things that I'd heard. Over the years, there were two people I'd made pretty mad at me: Bob Ball, the leader of the liberals, and David Stockman, the whiz kid of the conservatives. They obviously held no great affection for me.

The Administration probably had its misgivings, too. Perhaps they saw me as a loose cannon. There was some history to back them up on this. After all, I had resigned twice from the Social Security Administration and made a loud noise when I did it. The first time (see Chapter Seven) I pointed an accusing finger at Ball, and the second time (reported in Chapter One) I slammed Stockman. I don't think they wanted me in the room with them.

They met in Blair House, which is across Pennsylvania Avenue from the White House, and is where President Truman lived during the months it took to rebuild the inside of the executive mansion. Blair House serves as the official guest residence of the President. It was right around the corner from my office.

Greenspan told me what they were doing in these meetings. And what he didn't tell me I could figure out when they sent out requests for technical information or to have some numbers crunched.

In the time since the commission's public failure in November to now, I had been fielding calls daily from the news media. The networks, the big newspapers and the wire services all wanted to know what was going on. I would tell them that there were still talks, but I didn't have any progress to report. I didn't tell them that the talks were going on in secret meetings just a few doors down the street and around the corner from where I was sitting.

I didn't lie.

That would have been pointless and stupid. Spencer Rich, a reporter for *The Washington Post,* was writing about the meetings as they happened. "Leaders of the President's advisory commission on Social Security held secret talks yesterday," began a story that he had in the January 9 edition of the paper.

Some secret! Rich even listed all the people who attended the meeting, which, by the way, failed to produce an agreement for boosting the payroll tax.

Within a week, though, they put together a package that everybody agreed on in that group. We had run the figures on it, and it would do the job both short-range and long-range, with the long-range situation handled — this was the grand compromise — in either of two ways. It could be handled by a higher tax rate, beginning in 2010, or by raising the retirement age gradually beginning about 20 years hence.

Short-range, everybody agreed what to do about raising taxes and cutting benefits, so that was what you might call a true compromise: about half of what one wanted, and half of what another wanted. Even with that there were matters of definition. Is an income tax on benefits a true tax, or is it a reduction in benefits? Also, how should extension of coverage to new employment groups be considered? For the long-range, the group agreed on a financing plan which was more weighted toward raising taxes than cutting benefits, about a 7 to 1 split. But this only covered part of the long-range needs of the program; the rest was going to be left up to Congress. The short-range finances were handled 70 percent by revenue increases and 30 percent by benefits cuts. In general, I thought it was fair.

So as Saturday, January 15, rolled around, this group continued its closed-door work. They were close, and it looked as though this was going to go. Members of the commission had been told to stand by in case they had to be called into session quickly. This was also our second deadline. By law and presidential order, we were to vanish at midnight. During the day, Reagan signed one more single-sentence executive order. He gave us five more days.

Late in the afternoon, they did it.

The commissioners who'd been cooling their heels around town were summoned to Lafayette Square that evening. They knew that the Blair House meetings were going on, but they were good soldiers and didn't let their feelings over being left out dictate their behavior.

It was about six o'clock and dark outside when Greenspan called them to order. This townhouse that once seemed so spacious now was a tight fit as onlookers and reporters strained to wedge themselves through the doorways. These houses are really just two high-ceilinged rooms on each floor, a front room and a back room, and a vestibule and stairway.

Once everything got quiet, Greenspan turned to me and asked me to explain what was in the package. In a sense, this may have seemed like an unreasonable request since he was in the room where it was put together, and I was around the corner and a few doors down the street. I'd had some time to look at it and already was pretty familiar with its details, because I'd had to supply the working group with cost figures for various aspects of what they were doing. Besides, there weren't really any surprises here. It was pretty much a cut-and-paste job, taking pieces of one proposal or another and putting them together.

One of the most important things that the commission did was what it didn't do. It didn't change the basic structure of Social Security. On that they were unanimous. "The National Commission considered, but rejected, proposals to make the Social Security program a voluntary one, or to transform it into a program under which benefits are a product exclusively of the contributions paid, or to convert it into a fully-funded program, or to change it to a program under which benefits are conditioned on the showing of financial need," the commission said in its report to the President.

Here are the highlights of what was done:

(1) New civilian federal employees would be part of the Social Security system. State and local governments whose employees had been covered by Social Security on an elective basis could not decide to drop out of the system in the future. Also, employees of non-profit charitable, educational, and religious organizations would be covered compulsorily.

(2) Cutting off "windfall" benefits to people who spent most of their working lives in jobs not covered by Social Security, but who later become eligible for Social Security retirement benefits because of a relatively short time spent in a job covered by the system. An example of this would be a government employee who spent 30 years on the job without putting a dime into Social Security. This person then leaves government service and gets a job for 10 years working as a relatively-low paid store clerk. In addition to the government pension, this person would get an inordinately high benefit from Social Security. This recommendation sought to end this.

(3) Imposing an income tax on half of the Social Security benefits of someone with income of over $20,000 a year or a couple with over $25,000 a year.

(4) Delaying the date of the automatic cost-of-living increases from July to January, putting them on a calendar-year basis.

(5) Moving up the planned tax increases already in the law to help build up the fund. For 1984 this would raise the Social Security tax from 5.4 percent each for the employer and employee to 5.7 percent, the rate that wasn't supposed to take effect until a year later. However, the employee rate — by a neat bit of political footwork — would really stay at 5.4 percent for 1984 because the 0.3 percent increase would be a credit, paid from the General Treasury. The tax would rise again to 6.06 percent in the late 1980s and level off at 6.2 percent in 1990 and thereafter.

(6) Raising the tax on the self-employed to equal what would otherwise have been paid in employer and employee contributions. Under existing law, the self-employed paid just 75 percent of that amount. To take some of the sting out of this, and be consistent with the plan for employers, the self-employed would be able to take an income-tax deduction for one-half of the Social Security tax.

These and other provisions took care of the short-range problem and covered about two-thirds of what we projected to be the system's long-range financial needs, carrying it on a financially sound basis for the next 75 years.

The members couldn't agree on how to take care of this remaining one-third, so they decided to boil it down to two proposals and let Congress sort it out. One proposal was to start raising the retirement age gradually at some point decades hence, and the other was a 0.46 percent tax increase each on the employer and employee beginning in the year 2010.

All of this was considered to be part of a "consensus package," and I took half an hour to explain it to the commission and talk about how it worked, followed by a short discussion.

Then Greenspan, who for all these months had kept these people from going for each other's throats and had carefully avoided having them solidify their positions, called for a vote. The time had come.

The vote was 12 to 3, with Armstrong, Archer, and Waggonner — all conservatives — dissenting. The liberals and seven of the conservatives voted together. Reagan and House Speaker O'Neill immediately endorsed it. The deal was done.

By and large, Congress went along with the commission's package and took the option of raising the retirement age gradually to 67 by the year 2027, beginning the rise in 2003.

As Greenspan said, nobody liked the entire package. There was something in there for everybody to dislike. They just had to put something together to fill the actuarial job of keeping the system in operation through the 1980's and beyond. There, as with a collective bargaining agreement, you can't say that one side won, and one side lost. Both sides won, and both sides lost.

Of course, the dissenters wrote opinions explaining their disagreement. Armstrong, for example, didn't like raising taxes and had said all along that this was non-negotiable with him.

"There are other flaws in the commission recommendations and, to be fair, a number of good points as well," Armstrong wrote. "Overall, however, I cannot escape the conclusion that the plan needs much improving. Whether this will happen remains to be seen. At least one White House insider is freely predicting quick legislative approval with few, if any, changes. He points out that a lot of 'heavyweights' already are backing the package. He could be right.''

Even those who backed the plan found points that they had to disagree with. Kirkland wrote a dissent over bringing public employees into the Social Security program. He had to walk a fine line, and he did. Social Security is sacred to organized labor, but at the same time Kirkland was hearing the outcry from the public employee unions, who didn't like the idea of being forced into the program. He had to stick up for them without attacking Social Security. Basically, he wanted to make sure that their pension benefits would not be reduced and that they were not being financially penalized.

In all, there were 11 dissenting opinions, objecting to this or that feature of the plan, and every member of the commission signed at least one of them. There were things in there that were just abhorrent to Claude Pepper, and although he did join in a couple of dissenting opinions on Medicare cost estimates and on issues of concern to women, he went along with the plan.

He immediately sent a ''dear colleague'' letter to House Democrats urging them to support the commission's suggestions. ''I believe that this agreement is fair and responsible and will help the Congress and the President avoid a protracted political battle, one which might further erode the confidence of the American people in the Social Security system,'' Pepper wrote.

''All of us on the commission had to make sacrifices and concessions for the benefit of achieving an agreement,'' Pepper further wrote. ''They are a small price to pay for achieving a bipartisan agreement...''

He ended with a particularly eloquent passage: ''One message should ring loud and clear through all of the discussion. The Social Security system is here with us to stay. It is one of America's proudest achievements.''

On the day after the final meeting, Greenspan was equally eloquent in an interview on CNN: "None of this is any good except the conclusion."

If the commission had failed altogether, it would have been entirely up to Congress to do something about the problem because by June or July, the checks would not have gone out on time. It's completely hypothetical, but I believe that Congress' immediate solution would have been to find a way to borrow some money to keep the system afloat until a more permanent fix could be made. In other words, the system would have been left on the same kind of life-support system that had allowed it to function for the past year.

That's no way to run things, but it beats the alternative. It may sound funny, but it's not hard to imagine the riots that could come from a sudden shutdown of the Social Security system.

If you don't believe the elderly are capable of this, take a look at what happened to Dan Rostenkowski just a few years ago, when senior citizens surrounded his car and pounded on the hood to show their displeasure at having to pay rather modest premiums for catastrophic health insurance. Rostenkowski, a burly, gravel-voiced Democrat from Chicago is used to rough politics, but as chairman of the House Ways and Means Committee, he wasn't used to being treated like that. This single incident did much to persuade Congress to repeal that whole program.

So once the commission had done its work, we pulled it together into a report that was run off in a matter of hours. The White House did this for us, so we didn't even have to wait for our turn at the Government Printing Office.

On January 20, our third deadline and Ronald Reagan's second anniversary as President, the report was issued [2].

On January 21, my wife Rudy and I threw a party at our own expense at the elegant townhouse in celebration of the event. Many of the commissioners came, as well as the staff, the top officials of the Social Security Administration, and our own two sons and their wives. I was most surprised and pleased to be presented with a lead-crystal piece of art — the Excalibur Sword Embedded in the Rock. And Trowbridge, in presenting this ever-to-be treasured memento, extravagantly said that I was the only one who could have accomplished the "impossible" feat of achieving a consensus package.

Then we closed down the office and said our goodbyes.

And, at age 70, I was out of work again.

This time, it felt pretty good!

Epilogue

After this exciting and productive time, I did not go home and spend my time in a rocking chair on the front porch. Rather, I kept up to date with Social Security and Medicare experince and legislative changes, wrote papers, testified before Congress, and undertook technical assistance missions to other countries (see Chapter 8). Also, I had continuing consulting connections with several organizations, including the employee benefits firm of William M. Mercer, Inc., the National Association of Life Underwriters, and The Seniors Coalition. One of my most interesting activities was as a visiting professor for three weeks in 1990 at Nankai University in Tianjin, China. I also have the interesting work of being on the boards of trustees of two mutual funds — one of the American Association of Retired Persons and the other of the North American Security Life Insurance Company.

CHAPTER THREE

MY EARLY YEARS

My grandfather was a big, bald, humorless, scary man with a little moustache. But he was rich, so we lived with him.

Julius Hirsh was my mother's father, a self-made man, who made his fortune by knowing how to get into the textile business and kept his money by knowing when to get out.

If he had a sense of humor when he came to America in the 1860's, he might have lost it in Tennessee. That's where the Klan hanged him because he was a Jew. A sympathetic Black man cut him down and saved his life. The incident left Grandfather with a facial tic and a deep sense of gratitude to Black people. He built a small church for them, known as Hirsh's Chapel, in Somerville, a small town about 35 miles east of Memphis.

He left the South and had a small factory in Philadelphia that made knitted women's underwear. They were heavy, long, cotton drawers, and it's no wonder women wanted to wear something else. Grandfather knew the market was turning to silk and lighter cotton, so he sold out and pretty much retired. His only business after that was to get up every day, put on a suit, and go see his broker. He speculated in cotton futures and did well.

This carried us through the Depression, something we read about but didn't experience. His investments were safe; they survived the market crash and prospered in the worst of times.

My father, Laurence B. Myers, was just the opposite. He was a nice guy, but broke. He was smart, a graduate of Lehigh University, a civil engineer by training. But he never had any real money, his business ventures fizzled, and he had to put up with the humiliation of living with his wife's parents.

They never let him — or me, for that matter — forget whose house we were living in.

If my grandfather ruled the house, and he did, my mother, Edith Hirsh Myers, ran the place. In many ways they were very much alike. They liked taking charge.

My mother was a very outgoing person, and very strong-minded. I guess you would say she was opinionated. She had ideas, and that's the way things should be. She wasn't a feminist or a suffragette, but when she knew something, she just knew it.

Mother, for example, had decided that Dad's father, Solomon Herman Myers, was the youngest officer in the Confederate Army. There was no telling her any differently. In her mind he was a colonel and a gentleman of the South.

He was anything but.

Solomon was a Jewish immigrant from Bavaria, who came to America in 1860 when he was 15, following in the footsteps of his older brother, Abraham, according to a history compiled by his synagogue and my cousin Jack Myers. Abraham was a peddler traveling a route in northern Virginia, and after arriving in this country, Solomon got a peddler's route in southern Pennsylvania, the Shenandoah Valley, and the northern part of Virginia.

It was there that the two brothers found themselves when the Civil War started. Abraham joined the infantry to guard the wharves in Alexandria, and Solomon, who owned a horse, signed up with the 62nd Virginia Mounted Infantry. He probably fought at the second battle of Bull Run and the battle of Antietem.

Solomon's military career lasted just a little over two months. He signed up at the end of August 1862, and by early November he was a deserter. In April 1864, he re-joined the Confederate cause, this time with the 23rd Virginia Cavalry. The following November, Private Myers was captured during the bloody Shenandoah Campaign and was released at New Market, Va., on April 14, 1865, the same day Abraham Lincoln was assassinated.

Solomon went to Philadelphia, where he boarded with his brother until sometime in the 1870's. By that time he had become a citizen, and in 1876 he married Selina Kohn. My father, the fourth of their six children, was born December 23, 1885.

I don't know the particulars of his financial circumstances, but Dad was able to get himself a scholarship to Lehigh University, starting a family tradition of attending that school which endures to this day. (My granddaughter, Julie, is in the class of 1993.)

He arrived at Lehigh in 1903, the year his father died, and he graduated in 1907, the year his mother died. Dad seems to have been pretty well liked. His yearbook called him Larry. (Later in life his friends were to call him Laurie.)

"Larry has always been a good student and can chuck a good bluff if necessary," his senior yearbook said. "He also found time for athletics, having played a strong game at 'out home' on the Lacrosse team."

Four years after leaving school, he and my mother were married at the Mercantile Club in Philadelphia on November 22, 1911.

They were living in Lancaster, Pa., a year later, when I was born on Halloween — the first and only child. Dad was managing a small trolley line that ran from there to a resort town about a dozen miles away. When I was 3 years old we moved back to Philadelphia and into the house of my maternal grandparents. Dad had taken a job in Dover, Del., where he was managing an electric power utility. He had a car, but it was a 75-mile commute — still long even by today's standards — so he kept an apartment in Dover and drove back to Philadelphia on weekends. Dad and I didn't do a lot together, but he did take me to Dover with him sometimes for a couple of nights at a stretch.

Dad and Mother got along well and seemed to genuinely like each other. But being out of the house was probably something of a relief for him. My grandfather had a low opinion of Dad, compared with his views on the spouses of my mother's brother and her sister.

At the time we were living in the Mount Airy section of Philadelphia, and, at some point, I guess they figured our living arrangement with my grandparents was going to be permanent. Grandfather bought 1 3/4 acres in Elkins Park, north of Philadelphia, and built a house there. It was a large stone building with enough room for two families to stay out of each other's way. My grandparents lived in one wing, and we lived in another. There were even quarters for two servants. There was also a large greenhouse, where my folks raised orchids (partly as a hobby and partly commercially).

I didn't have any chores around the house. The cook made the meals, the maid kept everything clean, and the gardener kept the lawn nice. I never learned how to make a bed or wash a dish until I was in the Army, where the higher-ups decided these were skills I needed to help win the war.

Mother earned her keep by taking charge of the household. She supervised the servants, did the buying, paid the bills, kept the books, and planned the meals. Grandfather had certain demands, and she kept to them. Dinner had to be at six. The menu was set in stone. One night was brisket and string beans. On Sunday there was roast beef.

My grandmother, Sarah, wasn't much for details, so it was fine with her if someone else wanted to keep track of all this. That just meant Grandmother didn't have to be bothered.

Grandmother (as well as my mother and father) played golf — not too well — and I often caddied for her. My grandfather's entertainment was pinochle. He played on Sunday afternoons with old friends, and sometimes he took me along to "observe."

There were a few kids in the neighborhood to play with, mostly the children of servants at the neighboring estates. The lawns were big enough that we could get up a good game of football or baseball.

I was a serious kid. I did my work in school, I did what I was told, and I tried to stay out of the path of the grown-ups. No one had to tell me to do my homework.

It was at an early age that I decided I liked math. It was logical and tidy. It gave answers. It was predictable. All through school, my math grades were pretty good, mostly A's. But put a pencil in my hands, and I was all thumbs. My penmanship was lousy; I got F's. My drawing wasn't much better.

Dad was good at this, though. It sort of goes with being an engineer. You have to be able to draw plans, but his talent was more than just putting straight lines on a blueprint. He would illustrate his letters with little cartoons. Sometimes they were funny, and they were always artistic.

Dad used to write to Mother a lot, and I think she got a kick out of his letters, but she didn't keep them. They were hers, and they were private. And besides, she was a real stickler for neatness. Once she was done with a letter, it wasn't a keepsake to her, it was clutter. She threw them away.

I have one letter he wrote to Mother: "We will be so happy when we are always together. It sounds almost too good to be true to be married to you, dearest."

Underneath this was a drawing he cryptically titled "Blessed Be the Tie that Binds." That didn't seem to have anything to do with the drawing, which showed silhouettes of three women in Victorian dresses and big hats with their skirts flapping in a high wind. It was quite detailed and very well done.

I couldn't begin to do that. But at some point, I had decided that I wanted to follow in Dad's footsteps. There was never much said about it, but I found myself set on a course that had me pointed toward Lehigh and a career in engineering. This made sense. I admired Dad, and besides it didn't look like I could do anything else. I excelled at math on through Cheltenham High School, but my grades in other subjects like English or Latin could be pretty bad.

I had to take a public speaking course in high school and was especially bad at that. I got an F. (Years later I tried without success to track down that teacher to remind him of my terrible grade and to tell him I later went on to make a pretty good living giving speeches and testifying before congressional committees.)

I guess you could say I was kind of a nerdy kid. I was tall and skinny and I wore glasses because my eyes were not straight (although operations I had in my teens corrected this). In high school I went out for basketball and wound up as captain of the chess team.

As I look back on my life now, one of the things I've liked best about it is the traveling that has taken me all over the world. My grandmother awakened this in me when she took me on my first trip to Europe in 1928. She had previously traveled widely on arranged tours.

I was in high school at the time, and travel to Europe was pretty rare. It was also slow. Charles Lindbergh was one of the few who'd made the hop in an airplane. The rest of us were still going by ship.

So my grandmother and I boarded a ship in New York, the Conte Biancamano, bound for the port of Naples. She handed the details of the trip over to me. I handled the luggage, got us from here to there, took care of hotels, and read maps. I liked the responsibility, and she liked not being bothered with it.

A 16-year-old might cringe at the thought of traveling with a grandparent. But I had a good time. The trip was an adventure, and Grandmother was fun. She was chatty and outgoing.

We were to take a similar trip two years later, this time to Germany, where we drove around the country, gazing at castles, visiting a couple of beer gardens, and dropping in on some relatives in Berlin. I took care of the details again and did the driving.

We were oblivious to the political rumblings going on in the country at the time. Even with the 20/20 vision of hindsight, I can't remember anything out of the ordinary.

At the end of that summer, more than 100 Nazis were elected to the Reichstag. But we saw no swastikas, no brownshirts, and no rallies. I was just a Jewish kid on vacation with his grandmother. Nobody bothered us.

On the first European trip in 1928 we headed north from Naples, touring Italy and eventually making our way to Paris. There we took the then-risky move of catching a plane to England. We then boarded a ship for the return to New York.

When we docked in New York, something seemed wrong. Somebody came aboard the boat and hustled us through customs real fast, so that we avoided the usual hassle of standing in line. It was obvious someone had used some influence.

When we finally got off the ship, Dad and Mother were there waiting for us. They had driven up from Elkins Park. Something about them seemed strange. They had news that we would talk about when we got home. That was about a two-hour drive, which we had to endure wondering what was wrong. Grandmother seemed especially upset. After we got home, they told me to make myself scarce, and they went into the living room with Grandmother.

Grandfather was dead. It had happened a little more than a week earlier. A heart attack, probably. The decision had been made not to contact us in Europe to break the news. That may seem kind of cold-hearted, but it was really clear-headed. There was nothing Grandmother or I could have done about it. Had we been standing next to a ship when we found out, it would still have taken a week to get back to New York. That would have been too late. The only thing they would accomplish by telling us would be to ruin the end of the trip and turn the Atlantic crossing into an endless ordeal.

My grandparents had never shown any affection for each other in public, so I don't know how closely attached they were. Kids don't pay much attention to that kind of thing anyway. But this was emotional whiplash, and my grandmother was devastated at the news that her life's companion was gone.

Perhaps adding to her grief was the fact that he had begged her not to go on the trip to Europe. He wasn't clear in his explanation, but he hadn't been feeling very well. Grandmother dismissed it with an "Oh, you'll be alright."

This incident was to be repeated 27 years later, when my own father died. I was in Peru at the time on business and returned to the news that he was gone.

I think Dad was a success, even if he didn't get rich. I wanted to be like him, so there was never any question about what I was going to do. It was as seamless as going from junior to senior in high school. I was going to Lehigh. Dad and I had made the 50-mile trip to Bethlehem, Pa., several times to see the school. He thought it was a great place, and by the looks of it, I agreed.

First, though, I had to get through my senior year. My grades were solid, and I got accepted to college. That summer I landed a job as a messenger at Tradesmen's National Bank in Philadelphia.

Grandfather had friends on the board of directors there. Even though he was gone now, some old strings got pulled, and I got on the payroll. It was an old, respected bank, with marble floors, vaulted ceilings, a sense of serenity, and light filtering through the huge windows. People were called mister.

This was the summer of 1929. Times had been good. Economically, the country had been on a binge, and it seemed that everybody had some money. A lot of them were playing the stock market on margin, and the market was acting funny now. There were rumblings coming from somewhere deep inside, sort of like earth tremors centered in a volcano that had been considered long extinct.

Everybody was talking about it, even my boss, the head messenger at the bank. I didn't really like him. He acted like a drill sergeant. Maybe it was because he was a grown man holding down a job that could be handled by a kid. Anyway, he was into the market, playing with fire, and he was worried. He didn't confide in me, but I remember hearing him talking to others about his investments.

It was a sign of the times. He probably got sucked under with everybody else when the market crashed that October. By then, I was at school.

In September, Dad and I packed my belongings into the trunk of his Velie, a pretty spiffy roadster with a top that came down and a rumble seat that popped up. It was just the two of us heading down the road.

After we got there and hauled my stuff up to my room, I went back out to the curb with him. This was going to be one of those father-son moments. There had never been anything between us but respect and affection. Still, we didn't communicate as well as I wish we had. There was a lot that didn't get said.

There were only a few words on this occasion, and I don't even remember what they were. I know he told me to do well.

Then he drove away.

The dorm, Taylor Hall, was a U-shaped, three-story building that had been built about the time Dad was a student there, although he had never lived in it. It was divided into five sections, each with its own entrance, and to get from one section to another you had to go outside and come back in.

This separation fostered a sense of camaraderie sort of like a fraternity with 24 fellows in it. The living arrangement wasn't too bad: a suite with two bedrooms and a sitting room for two guys. They still use this dorm, but now they've got the kids packed in there a little tighter, two to a bedroom and four to a suite.

But the physical arrangements didn't make as much of an impression on me as what was to follow. Lehigh had an interesting admissions philosophy — it was easy to get in and hard to stay. They flunked kids out, and they were proud of it. This was driven home in the first week I was there.

They gave us the usual yammer about the history of the university and what life was going to be like. We also got speeches on the virtues of diligent study and the dangers of alcohol and venereal disease (remember, penicillin did not yet exist outside the laboratory).

At some point during this indoctrination, they marched us into the local movie theater, I'm certain for the sole purpose of scaring the hell out of us. It worked.

It's a tried and true speech now, but it was brand new to me when I heard it. Somebody got up on the stage, perhaps the dean of students. At one point in his talk he stopped and said, "Look at the fellow on the right, then turn around and look at the fellow on the left of you. Only one of you three will graduate from Lehigh."

This was no bluff. Only one-third of the entering class would end up graduating.

So I was scared silly when I walked into a classroom for the first time. I tried to study a lot and work hard. I started getting grades, and I saw I was going to make it. My first semester was my poorest, but I passed everything.

One of the first academic casualties was a kid from Scranton, the heart of Pennsylvania's coal country. This kid was poor, the son of a miner, and we had become friends. He tried hard, but he couldn't make it. They flunked him out after the first semester. He was heartbroken, but he had lots of company. It was a rough time.

I was holding my own in the classroom, but there were other problems. Roommates were pretty much the luck of the draw the first year. You took whomever they gave you. Mine was an anti-Semite from New Jersey.

He made it no secret that he didn't like being paired up with a Jewish kid. He didn't like me, and I didn't like him back. But we were stuck with each other, and over time the wall of prejudice began to soften.

The wall was breached, finally, when he ran into trouble with his math. He was on my turf now. Letting him sink was tempting, but in the end I helped him. We got to be friendly. But at the first opportunity, I put in a bid for another roommate for the next year.

Lehigh was serious about football. We had to go to the games. But at the time they weren't serious about recruiting good players. The team was lousy. The games were fun anyway, though. As freshmen, we went decked out in our dinks, the goofy brown-and-white beanies we had to wear everywhere. It even had a winter model, which was sort of a knit cap. They wear like iron. I've still got mine and still wear it on cold nights when I take our dog, Jamie, out for a walk.

Lehigh had a very good wrestling team, though, and I went out for it. I never really had any previous training, if you don't count the spontaneous wrestling meets in the dorm when we'd get tired of hitting the books and started hitting each other. I didn't get stuck on the chess team, but I didn't make the wrestling team either. They did let me stay on the squad, so I got to wrestle with members of the team and — best of all — I got free towels in the gym. Hey, a nickel was a nickel. (And the wrestling training came in handy later. I won the dormitory championship in my weight class at the University of Iowa later, and then the District of Columbia A.A.U. championship when I arrived in Washington.)

Social life otherwise was pretty dull. Girls were scarce. Lehigh, at that time, was not coed. There was a Catholic Church in town where you could go for the occasional bingo game and dance. And there were speakeasies where you could go get a beer.

The mayor of Bethlehem had a pretty enlightened attitude about beer drinking. He was for it, Prohibition or not. These Pennsylvania Dutch people liked their beer. Breweries were operating pretty much in the open. I don't know why they didn't get shut down, but they didn't. The mayor said that as long as the speakeasies stuck to beer, rather than hard liquor, they'd stay open. Everybody seemed to get along.

But we weren't at Lehigh for the beer or the bingo. This was serious stuff, and we were expected to work pretty hard.

In engineering you carried an 18-hour load and could take an extra three hours if your marks were good enough. There also were labs, and they took lots of time. You went to school mornings, afternoons, and Saturday mornings as well.

After the first semester, when my grades were just so-so, I was able to do better. In the end, I made Phi Beta Kappa and Sigma Xi, something of the equivalent of Phi Beta Kappa in the scientific field. I ended up graduating sixth out of a class of some 200.

Before the first year was up, I knew I wasn't going to be a civil engineer like Dad. I didn't think the prospects were too good, and besides I wasn't too good at what they called engineering drawing, where you had to make sketches of the way a bridge or a road is built.

Figuring out what I wanted to be when I grew up was important, because at the end of the freshmen year we had to decide what kind of engineering courses we were going to take from then on. I didn't particularly like engineering, but I did like the math, so I picked engineering physics.

I stuck with this through my sophomore and junior years and eventually decided it had no future, at least not for me. Shows how much I knew! The guys who invented atomic energy came out of this line of schooling, so it might have been a pretty good career. But I didn't really like the labs.

Teaching was out. I liked to teach people, but taking education courses was a waste of time, and the kind of math courses you had to take to get a Ph.D. were too theoretical for my liking. I wanted something you could use, something where a question was asked and the numbers yielded an answer.

Whatever I was going to do, I'd have to do it quickly. Time was running out on college, and I wanted to graduate on time.

So in the summer of 1932, following my junior year, when I was home in Philadelphia, a friend of my parents — I think he was their insurance agent — suggested that I might like to be an actuary if I was good at math.

I didn't know what an actuary was.

This friend said, "I know an actuary at the Provident Mutual Life Insurance Co. in Philadelphia. Why doesn't he go talk to him?"

I went to talk to this fellow, Everett Armentrout, a qualified actuary. Like all other actuaries that I know, he was glad to talk to a prospective student. I know this may sound painfully dull to some people, but I was fascinated. This was the kind of math that I wanted all along. I didn't have to draw, I didn't have to teach, and I didn't have to wallow in theory.

This was numbers. Lots of them. If you manipulated them right, they could tell you the future, or at least give you an idea of its general direction. How long might people live 50 years from now? How much money might they be making? How might they be living?

The answers which these numbers give aren't firm, but it's better than guessing.

I was 20 years old and ready to take my actuarial exams. At the time there were a dozen of them. Some of them were on subjects I'd already studied, such as trigonometry, algebra, analytic geometry, and statistics. They also got into other courses, such as mathematical statistics, finance and insurance, insurance accounting, and law. And today they include something that didn't exist then: Social Security! Mr. Armentrout told me the exams were hard, but he encouraged me to take them.

I started shifting my elective courses around to accommodate this new-found vocation by taking more business administration courses. The chairman of the mathematics department was horrified when I told him I was going in for actuarial science.

That was heresy, blasphemy! He was a theoretical mathematician, and this very practical use of mathematics seemed to him to be not quite decent.

To add insult to injury, there was a math contest every month, and the prize was a book of the winner's choosing. I won the contest one month in my senior year, and the book I picked was on actuarial math. This professor didn't like my choice a bit, but he went along with it.

At that time, the math department offered courses in mathematics of life insurance, which is really actuarial science, and the mathematics of finance, or compound interest. There's a lot of mathematics there, but it's not complicated.

They gave these courses as electives for business administration students, and I signed up. And again my prof threw a fit.

"You shouldn't take those courses," he said. "They're too elementary. They're just meant for business administration students, not for math majors or math specialists."

I insisted and took them anyway. He was right. They were a snap because my eight fellow students, although not dummies, weren't math majors. It was very elementary actuarial science, and when I later went to the University of Iowa for an actuarial degree, I found out how elementary these courses had been. But it gave me a good taste of what actuarial math was about. As I say, I enjoyed taking them. It wasn't hard work, and I breezed through with A's.

Now I was ready to graduate with a degree in engineering and a hankering for actuarial science. Suddenly, the Depression that had left me alone all these years was real. I needed a job, and I didn't have one. There weren't any to be had. I had taken four of the actuarial exams, passing two and failing two.

I was wondering what I was going to do, and my folks were wondering the same thing. Finally, they asked if I wanted to go back to school to be an actuary. There were only two places to go at the time, the University of Michigan and the University of Iowa. I applied to both and was accepted at both. But Iowa sweetened the pot and gave me a quarter-time assistanceship, so I was off for the Midwest.

I had a car that my folks had given me for a graduation present. It was a spiffy 1933 Chevrolet roadster with a rumble seat. It was brand new and cost about $600. I think it was some kind of deal my father had gotten as a commission on some engineering job that he did. They never told me too much, and I didn't think it was proper to ask them.

This assistanceship which I had at Iowa was supposed to be a big deal. I had to work 10 hours a week and got paid $225 a year, plus a two-thirds reduction in tuition. That made my tuition bill something like $20 a semester, and my parents paid that. The dorm room cost $50 a year, and meals in the cafeteria were 25 cents or so. That $225 wasn't nearly as small as it sounds today.

Iowa was good, but it didn't have as deep or lasting an effect on me as Lehigh did. I still have a great affection for the latter place. So much so that about half a century after I left, I jumped at the chance to go back and just take a look around.

It was in 1983, and a congressman had asked me to come to Bethlehem to talk to a town meeting about Social Security. I got there in the morning and had some time to kill. The congressman's staff asked if there was anything I wanted to do. I asked them to drive me to Lehigh, where I spent an hour just enjoyably walking up and down that mountain and seeing the place. It gave me a kick just being there.

Fifty years after the diploma, how do you explain something like this?

Well maybe it's like being in love with a woman. You don't always know quite why.

There was another time in my life that I felt something like that. It was when I fell for Ruth "Rudy" McCoy, who was arriving in Washington on a train from Pennsylvania to seek her fortune while I was still in the Midwest working on my degree.

If ever there was an argument for the need for the Social Security system, Rudy's family was it. She came from Bellwood, Pa., a gritty little town just east of Altoona. Rudy was the baby of a family of five children, three boys and two girls.

Her father, Samuel Kelly McCoy, was a dark-haired, blue-eyed Irishman, who loved to tell a story and sing a song. He also had the curse and would disappear for days on end when he took off on a binge that would probably end up with a fight. Sometimes he would land in jail, and as likely as not he would have lost something he needed, maybe an overcoat, maybe his false teeth. It was up to Rudy's mother to bail him out and try to put him back together.

Her mother, Florence Dengate McCoy, was an understandably nervous woman. If she wasn't trying to repair the damage from Samuel's last disappearance, she was trying to prevent the next one, or at least postpone it as long as she could. When he was home and sober, she made sure the house stayed quiet, hoping that the tranquility would keep him from taking off again.

The family was always broke, and Rudy's mother was a fanatic about putting money away. She had to be because she never knew when Samuel was going to take off or lose his job.

The best job he ever had was working for the Pennsylvania Railroad as an air brake inspector, and Florence was proud of him because he had to work hard to get that, even taking a correspondence course. Like everything else about him, though, it didn't last. He got fired. He was drinking.

He wound up going to work for a grocery store in town, making deliveries in a Ford Model A truck, and he even let Rudy drive it. On May 24, 1926, there was a knock at the door.

Samuel had been in a wreck, and he was dead. Rudy was just 12 years old.

Now the family didn't even have his sporadic income. There was no such thing as Social Security, no survivors' benefits, no real welfare system. The choices were work, accept charity, or starve.

They went to work. Like people everywhere in those days, they were adaptable. They made do with whatever they could find, and they didn't complain about their lot.

"We ate an awful lot of mush and stuff made from cornmeal, but we never went hungry," Rudy says. "We didn't have much milk and not a whole lot to eat, but we kept well."

Rudy and her mother brought in $15 a month from cleaning the Lutheran church next door, and one of her brothers tended the furnace. This is where Rudy went to Sunday School. Her mother was a Methodist, but the Methodist Sunday School didn't appeal to her.

They didn't feel poor. Everybody else was pretty much in the same boat, and if anybody had anything, it seems that they helped somebody else along with it.

One fellow whose house they cleaned was a retired engineer for the Pennsylvania Railroad, and he helped Rudy's 18-year-old brother, Dick, get a job as a gandy dancer, using an iron bar to straighten the tracks. Dick was never to leave the railroad, and wound up working in the car repair shop in Altoona. The noise destroyed his hearing, but otherwise it was a pretty good living.

Rudy finished high school in Bellwood and went to business college in Altoona, where she spent a year and a half learning practical skills, such as shorthand, accounting, typing, and English. But when she finished school, she was kind of like me: a good education and no job. So she kept going, sort of as an unpaid teacher's aide. It helped hone her skills, so she was still sharp when the Civil Service exams were given for secretaries.

She first got a job writing checks for the Works Progress Administration in Altoona. It was horrible work, and it ruined her eyes. It was just a grind, check after check, and they had to go out on time, so there were some nights when she had to stay in Altoona at the YWCA because she got off work so late.

Rudy was angling for a job in Washington. She'd had enough of Bellwood and that part of Pennsylvania. To an outsider it was pretty, nestled in the mountains as it was. But the hard times made it kind of depressing. Houses didn't get painted, and the place started to look frayed around the edges and run down.

In 1934, she got her wish. A telegram arrived from Washington, two years after she'd taken her exam. It was from the Veteran's Administration, giving an address, a room number, and a date. It said be there at 9 a.m. The job paid the tidy sum of $1,440 a year, less a 15 percent reduction that all civil servants had to accept in those days. Still, that worked out to a little better than $100 a month. As it turned out, the job was in connection with the Civil Service Retirement System. Later the work (and Rudy, too) was transferred to the Civil Service Commission.

That beat the $7 a week she was pulling down working in the office of a chicken hatchery, and furthermore this was a chance to get out of Bellwood. She dove for it.

Her brother went with her to the trolley station where she went to Tyrone and caught a train for Washington. She wasn't afraid one bit. Rudy had been to Washington once on a high-school trip and decided that she wanted to come back. When she got to Union Station, she went to Traveler's Aid and made it over to the YWCA, at 11th and M streets, N.W.

Franklin D. Roosevelt had been in office for about a year and was trying to get the New Deal started. That meant paperwork for the government, and there were a lot of women like

Rudy who came to Washington around that time to help with the load. They were pretty much the same age because they had all just gotten out of business college, and they were from all over the country, from New York to California.

The YWCA, where a lot of them landed, was something like a barracks. There was a little privacy, however, with one's sleeping area separated from the next one by curtains.

The working conditions of her first job were an awful lot like her living conditions. She sat in a big room. Occasionally someone would call for her, and she would go take dictation. But there was no continuity, and nothing really to hook her interest. This was just a temporary job, a three-month assignment, and Rudy got the impression — correctly — that at the end of that time the government could toss her out as impersonally as it had brought her in.

She had arrived in February and wanted to go home for Easter that year, just taking an unpaid leave. She was told that if she left, there'd be no job when she came back. So at the age of 21 and having been in Washington all of a couple of months, she decided she'd get someone to use some influence for her. Rudy learned fast.

Without an appointment she went up to Capitol Hill and strolled into the office of Jim Davis, a senator from Pennsylvania. She explained her problem, and within a week she had a permanent job, and a better one, although at the same pay.

Being a single woman in Washington in the 1930's was a ball, and Rudy had the time of her life. It seemed as though there was always a dance or a party going on somewhere, and although she didn't know how to dance when she got off the train from Pennsylvania, she learned that fast, too.

So it was at a dance, of course, that she and I met in October 1934. I had been in Washington only a couple of weeks and was staying at the YMCA. The dance was a mixer for the

YWCA and the YMCA. I was smitten right away, and over time we became steady dinner companions. Rudy was vivacious, witty, intelligent, and a real good-looker — all packed into 5 feet tall and 98 pounds. A real "fire cracker" born on the Fourth of July!

There were a few awkward moments with our families. My folks were put off because Rudy wasn't Jewish, and her folks were bothered because I was. That was a pointless exercise because in 1950 I would convert to Christianity and join the Lutheran Church.

I was serious about her right away. She was serious about having a good time. In fact, she was still engaged to someone else at the time, a boy from Bellwood who had given her a ring on the first Christmas after she'd come to Washington. She took the ring off when she was out on the town.

She wore it when she went on dates with me.

Rudy dated around a lot, even after she and I started going out. But she always told me when she had a date and would mention the fellow's name. Thank goodness it was always somebody different.

One of Rudy's most interesting activities was being in the casts of "little theaters." I would usually go to her rehearsals and performances — some might says so as to keep the stage-door Johnnies away. At the same time, I used these hours of waiting to good advantage by studying for the actuarial exams.

Our courtship lasted four years, and we were married on December 20, 1938.

My route to Washington — and to Rudy — had been somewhat roundabout.

Before I graduated from Iowa in 1934, I had passed another two actuarial exams, now making four. Now I had a master's degree and four exams under my belt, but the Depression was every bit as bad as a year earlier, and I still had no job.

You didn't have to be too smart to see that this was coming, so for weeks before graduation, I'd been writing to insurance companies. In those days, that was the only place for an actuary to work.

Nothing.

I went back to Philadelphia to Provident Mutual, where I'd first heard of actuarial science. They were very nice and said things like, "Gee you've got a good record, good school, good marks, and some success on the actuarial exams. We just don't have any openings at the moment."

I got a good reception everywhere I went, but no job. I took a trip to New York, went to some of the large insurance companies there. They were nice, generally speaking, except for one incident that I'll get to in a minute. They just said, "We don't have any jobs, but we'll keep your name. It's a great profession, and we need actuaries, but we just don't have any openings."

The one occasion that wasn't so good was when I went to Metropolitan Life, which was then the largest company, and had an interview with a woman whose name mercifully escapes me now. I think she was in personnel and wasn't an actuary. Evidently I didn't interview so well. I was introspective, not greatly outgoing, shy, and I didn't like going around asking for a job. I still don't know for sure what I did wrong.

But after the interview she proceeded to tell me that I was never going to be an actuary, and I might as well forget about it. She said I didn't have the right personality.

Personality? Oh, come on! We actuaries are not known for our humor, but even *we* tell jokes about that. Here are a couple of them. Actuaries are people who don't have personality enough to be accountants. Or an actuary is just like a computer except an actuary doesn't have a heart.

Those knock 'em dead at conventions.

(As an aside, it turned out that my fellow actuaries thought quite differently than she: 36 years later they honored me by electing me president of both the Society of Actuaries and the American Academy of Actuaries.)

At any rate she proceeded to give me this friendly advice that sort of dampened my spirits. Later on I surely would have liked to drop her a little note. Actually, I have had some very good dealings with the Metropolitan Life, because some of their actuaries were originally very active in the field of Social Security and very supportive of it. Reinhard Hohaus, who eventually was their senior vice president and chief actuary, was very helpful to me in my career, and there are other actuaries at the Met with whom I've been very good friends.

After this rather unhappy experience, I went back to Philadelphia. One day in the summer of 1934, I got a letter from my professor at Iowa, Henry Lewis Rietz, who was one of two top early actuarial educators in the country. (The other one was at Michigan. That's why those two schools were where they were. The schools were developed because of the men.) Professor Rietz was a mathematician, but he became interested in actuarial math and wrote many books on the subject. He was the one to whom I was the research assistant.

Unfortunately I cannot find his letter, but I remember what it said. It was a little unflattering. In essence it said, "Dear Bob: I am on a committee of actuarial consultants to the Committee on Economic Security." [This was the group that made the study setting up Social Security. I didn't know what it was then.] "The committee is looking for a junior actuary for a temporary job in Washington, D.C., and I am writing to you because you are my nearest graduate to Washington."

So my principal qualification seemed to be that I lived near Washington and therefore would be willing to take a six-week temporary job.

I came to Washington, and the rest, as they say, is history.

CHAPTER FOUR

IN THE BEGINNING

Going to work for Social Security when I did was like going to work at Sears before Roebuck or Merrill before Lynch.

It may seem odd to say now, but at the time I didn't have the sense that I was part of anything momentous. It was a job and a temporary one at that. Six weeks and I'd probably find myself back on the street. That wasn't a nice place to be in 1934. There were men out there selling apples.

Of course, I could always have gone back home to Philadelphia, so there was no danger of my starving. But I had all this education, and I wanted to use it. That's what excited me about landing even a temporary job as a junior actuary with the Committee on Economic Security.

I had gone to Washington in mid-September for an interview with Edwin Witte, the executive director of the committee. Witte had been a college professor at Wisconsin, and he looked like it. He was a stocky, balding, round-headed fellow, whose job was to make sense out of what was — up that point — a half-baked idea by President Roosevelt.

Maybe that's what made him seem gruff, or maybe I was just overly nervous. Anyway, we didn't talk very long, and he offered me a job. He said, "What salary do you expect?"

I knew what some of my classmates were getting in their first jobs out of school as actuaries. One fellow went to work for Prudential Life at $100 a month.

"A hundred dollars a month," I said.

"Oh, no. We can't pay you that," Witte said. "That's too little. That's less than stenographers and typists are getting."

He offered me the princely sum of $1,800 a year. Well, almost. At the time, because of the Depression, government employees had taken pay cuts, which were being phased out from year to year. The pay cut in effect at the time was 10 percent, so my annual salary was $1,620. That doesn't sound like a lot, and really it wasn't. But it was more than what a lot of people were making, which was nothing. In fact, for people who were working, it was well above average. From 1929 to 1932, the earnings of an average worker had dropped from $1,475 to $1,199, so I was doing pretty well. My first day on the job was September 23, 1934.

Witte was nothing if not fair. A week earlier he'd hired at the same salary one of his former students, Wilbur Cohen, as sort of an aide-de-camp and research assistant. Wilbur and I immediately struck up a friendship that was to last a lifetime and would endure despite our political differences of opinion. In a little more than 30 years, I would find myself working for Wilbur when President Johnson appointed him Secretary of Health, Education, and Welfare.

I had been to Washington before. Like lots of kids, I came here on a school trip, when we arrived from Elkins Park on a train. More recently I'd been here fishing for a job. The Acacia Mutual Life Insurance Co. had sent me a letter when I came back from Iowa. It was the largest life insurance company headquartered in Washington, a city not noted for large life insurance companies. (The company's still around and doing well, and still headquartered near the Capitol.) Someone at the company had seen my name on a list when I passed two more of my actuarial exams. I was summoned for an interview but didn't get the job. It was just after that when the letter came from my old professor in Iowa suggesting I get in contact with the newly formed committee.

FDR had decided that the government owed something to its citizens, to provide, if it could, a cradle-to-grave shield against calamity. On June 8, 1934, he delivered the following message to Congress:

"Our task of reconstruction does not require the creation of new and strange values. It is rather the finding of the way once more to known, but to some degree forgotten, ideals and values. If the means and details are in some instances new, the objectives are as permanent as human nature.

"Among our objectives I place the security of the men, women, and children of the Nation first.

"This security for the individual and for the family concerns itself primarily with three factors. People want decent homes to live in; they want to locate them where they can engage in productive work; and they want some safeguard against the misfortunes which cannot be wholly eliminated in this man-made world of ours."

Three weeks later, the President signed an executive order establishing the Committee on Economic Security to deal with this third point. It was chaired by Labor Secretary Frances Perkins, and its other members were Treasury Secretary Henry Morgenthau Jr., Attorney General Homer Cummings, Agriculture Secretary Henry A. Wallace, and Federal Emergency Relief Administrator

Harry L. Hopkins. It was to develop a program that would address unemployment, health care, child welfare, and old-age security. The mandate was broad, and the time was short. Roosevelt's order said the report had to be on his desk no later than December 1, 1934.

FDR had pushed for this sort of thing as governor of New York, where he called for a system of old-age insurance. And in meeting with the Committee on Economic Security, he floated the notion of every child being given an "insurance policy" at birth to provide protection against the misfortunes of life.

Very quickly, though, "insurance" was a word that was dropped. This was because there was nothing in the Constitution that gave the government the power to insure anything. The Supreme Court was full of old Republicans who were taking a rather literalist view of the Constitution, so calling this insurance, even though that's what it was, might give some of these justices the opening they needed to declare it unconstitutional.

One other way the Roosevelt Administration tried to tip-toe around the constitutional trip wires was in how the system was financed. In the final law, the collection of Social Security taxes and the payment of Social Security benefits were contained in separate titles, and in essence were separate laws. It was feared that tying the two together in one law would not pass constitutional muster. Indeed, the court had struck down a similar kind of financing scheme that involved an excise tax on cotton processors. The money from this tax was paid to cotton growers not to grow cotton. The court ruled that the tax wasn't really a tax, but was an unconstitutional means of imposing federal regulation.

So Social Security kept the flow of money in and the flow of money out separated. It didn't say that these taxes would provide these benefits. It just worked out by the purest of coincidences that the taxes were on the wages of the same people whose wages counted as credits toward benefits. (This whole ruse was dropped several years later when the Supreme Court ruled Social Security constitutional.)

However they wanted to categorize it, the idea didn't really get a name until sometime the following year. There is some historical debate over the origins of the term "social security." It is widely considered to be an American invention. It is, but its origin may be traced to South America, where Simon Bolivar used it in 1819: "The system of government most perfect is that which produces the greatest amount of happiness possible, the greatest amount of social security, and the greatest amount of political stability."

My friend Arthur Altmeyer turned up this quote from Bolivar after years of bragging that we had invented the term, although not the idea, of social security. Altmeyer, a brilliant labor economist and public servant who would serve as Chairman of the Social Security Board and later as Commissioner for Social Security, had this brought to his attention while he was working on a project in Bogota, Colombia, and he gave due credit ever since to the Great Liberator for coining the phrase. However, we in the United States have given it its modern meaning, and it is that meaning that has since been adopted by virtually every nation around the world.

Besides, FDR liked it because it sounded good. It sort of rolls off the tongue. In modern times, it seems to have surfaced in 1933 when an old-age lobbying group incorporated it into its name, the American Association for Social Security. The bill that was originally drafted and sent to Congress was called the Economic Security Bill, but Altmeyer figured that sometime during the hearings on the matter people just started calling it "social security." By the time Congress was through with the legislation, it had a new name — the Social Security Act.

Witte's immediate problem, however, wasn't pondering over a name. It was finding a place to work and hiring a staff.

He figured that 25 people would do nicely, and the President had given him all of $87,500 to pay for the operation. That money had to come from the budget for Hopkins' agency. These estimates — as government guesswork often does — came in on the low side. At the height of activity in late 1934 the committee had 100 employees, according to Witte, and by the time the work was done, it had cost $145,000. That was still something of a bargain, considering what we've derived from it.

For quarters we were put up in the Walker-Johnson Building, which is where Hopkins' agency was situated. This was a decision brought on by necessity and politics. The first place that Witte looked was the Labor Department because, after all, Secretary Perkins was the chairwoman of the committee. But there was no room at Labor. Hopkins, who was on a trip to Europe, left instructions before his departure that the committee was to be quartered with his agency.

That, of course, raised a howl from the Labor Department, which complained that the committee ought to be on "neutral ground," according to Witte. So he went out and found room at the Commerce Department, but before he could move in, he was stopped on orders from the Labor Department. Secretary Perkins overruled the concerns of her assistants and told Witte to take the space that Hopkins offered. To do otherwise, she said, might have been seen as unfriendly.

The building, which is gone now, stood by the Corcoran Gallery of Art, about a block west of the White House grounds. It originally was an apartment building, where they broke out some walls and turned it into offices. Still, there were lots of little rooms — which is how a 22-year-old hireling like me wound up with an office pretty much to myself — and it seemed as though there were bathrooms everywhere.

The office was a fairly placid place. The people were studious — many of them were academics who had come to town to work on this project — and although we were laboring against a tight deadline, nobody seemed to be frantic. The work was divided into different fields. One field was old-age pensions, one was unemployment insurance, and another was health, involving various studies.

We did our work in relative and peaceful obscurity. People were not coming in off the street or writing us a lot of letters, asking what we were going to do about this problem or that. To the people in the rest of the country, what was going on in Washington must have seemed like a blur because there was so much of it.

One thing that did generate some mail, though, was the so-called Townsend plan. This was the brain child of a California physician, Dr. Francis E. Townsend, who proposed giving a $200 monthly pension to everybody in the country over age 60. The only string attached was they had to spend the money every month. They couldn't save it. This would, according to the good doctor, put money into the hands of the elderly and get it circulating in the economy all at the same time.

Townsend was offering to give the elderly roughly twice what the average wage earner in the country was making. In those desperate times, the Townsend Old Age Revolving Pension Plan caught on quickly, and Townsend Clubs sprung up across the country.

In his contemporaneous history of the 1930's *Since Yesterday* [5], historian Frederick Lewis Allen wrote:

"It was no smiling matter for the Democratic general staff that the number of Townsend Club members was conservatively estimated at 3 million, and that the movement, by the end of 1935, had gained at least 10 million supporters. Old Age, it appeared, must be served."

Years later, Frances Perkins said as much [12]:

"And then there was the Townsend plan which both drove us and confused the issue. Without the Townsend plan, it is possible that the old-age insurance system would not have received the attention which it did at the hands of Congress. However, to have accepted the Townsend plan would have been ridiculous and would have damaged the economy still further."

As I recall, some of the Townsend mail landed on Cohen's desk, and among his other jobs was trying to answer it.

I wasn't so much concerned with this, though. I was but a small cog in this machine. I enjoyed working with numbers and learning how to apply the actuarial science I'd learned in school to a real problem.

There were two actuaries on the staff, Otto Richter and W.R. Williamson. Richter was loaned by American Telephone & Telegraph Co. for this job. Actuaries were relatively rare and specialized, so it was unusual in those days for a company to have one of its own, but AT&T had its own big private pension plan. Williamson was loaned by The Travelers Insurance Company, and he later came back as the top actuary of the Social Security Board.

I worked entirely for Richter because Williamson was working on unemployment insurance, and Richter was working on pensions. In essence what I did was make computations by following his directions. Richter was a very nice fellow, a little introspective, which I guess most actuaries are. I liked him, and he seemed to like me alright. I didn't seem to do too many things that were wrong.

If this job were to have been done today, a lot of what I did would have been done by a computer. But there still would have been a need for a human around to supervise the machine.

What follows here is a short lesson in what an actuary does. This won't take long, and it won't be complicated.

Typical of the jobs I did was to make a population projection of the United States, starting off with the 1930 census that would show the population, male and female, separately by five-year age groups in various future years.

Actuaries deal a lot in death, so I spent a fair amount of time poring over mortality tables, showing year by year how many people were going to die. Through a series of mathematical formulas, I would apply this to the population, using death rates broken down by age and sex. The goal is to predict how many people in each age range will be alive during any given period. For example, I would start with the number of people between the ages of 25 and 29 in 1930. From that, I should be able to calculate how many people between the ages of 30 and 34 would be alive in 1935. I would keep doing this projection, five years at a whack, off into the future to the end of the century (although most other projections were just to 1980, which had been picked rather arbitrarily because it was a distant, round number).

That gives you how many people you're going to have alive and how many you're going to lose. Now you have to figure in how many new people you're going to get. Essentially that's through births, and, to a lesser degree, immigration. The number of births for 1930-34 was, more or less, a known figure. From that you can determine how many people at age 0 to 4 will be alive in 1935 and then project them out into the future until they die off, or you stop calculating.

But how do you figure the births for the future? Well, you kind of go at it backwards. First, you take a stab at what you think the total population will be for any year. Then you subtract the number of people you think are going to survive until then. The number that's left is how many people arrived. Another way to go at it is to use estimated fertility rates, so you have a number of ways to attack the same problem.

In 1934, this was done with clunky, slow, noisy, electric calculating machines, and we entered the results on large sheets of paper using sharp pencils. It took a while, and you usually had another human or two looking over your shoulder to check your work.

The end result yielded nifty tables of crisp, believable numbers. But as you have just seen, some of this — no, a lot of it — is based on guesswork. Hopefully, though, it's informed guesswork.

Sometimes you have to sit and ponder the future. Not the Buck Rogers kind of stuff, where you wonder if people are going to fly around with their own personal rocket packs or get beamed from one spot to another at the speed of a phone call. Today looks pretty much like yesterday, which looked pretty much like the day before. The future is just a continuation of the present.

The kind of future gazing I'm talking about involves considering the possibility of declines in mortality rates, advances in medical science, changes in human behavior, improvements in sanitation, increases in the standard of living, improved education, and so forth. In other words, you have to make some assumptions, but they have to be reasonable and have some basis in present fact, rather than fantasy or wishful thinking.

At the end of all of this, we projected that the population of the United States would level off at 151 million in 1990 and stay there until the end of the century. It's easy to laugh now and say we were off by "only" about 98 million. Bear in mind that there were lots of things that we couldn't predict, big things like World War II and the postwar baby boom.

You could rightfully wonder, then, what good did all of this tedious ciphering do if the numbers were so wrong. Let's look at another number, the number of people at least age 65. In

1934 we predicted that number would be 19.1 million in 1990. The actual number, as counted in the 1990 census, turned out to be 31.1 million.

So we were wrong again.

But what we were really trying to get at was not *how many* people would be 65 or older, but what *proportion* of the population this would represent. In 1930, for example, the population of the United States was 122.775 million and the number of people over 65 stood at 6.634 million. This meant that 5.4 percent of the U.S. population was at least 65 years old.

Based on our population projections, this proportion was going to rise steadily over the years. For 1940 we figured it at 6.3 percent. By 1970 it was to have hit 10.1 percent. For 1990 we pegged it at 12.65 percent. The actual proportion in 1990, according to the census, was 12.49 percent.

That's pretty good shooting.

There, that's what an actuary does.

This is more than an academic exercise, especially when you're dealing with old-age pensions. It's about the only way you have of figuring out what your costs are. In addition to the size of the benefits, the cost of a program such as Social Security depends on how many people are around to collect those benefits and how long they might live.

Another, and even better, indication of the value and potential reliability of actuarial cost estimates is to consider the 1935 estimate of the cost of the Social Security program in 1980. It is far better to consider such cost in terms of percentage of taxable payroll, rather than in inflation-affected dollars. Such estimated cost was 9.65 percent, and the actual experience for Old-Age and Survivors Insurance (the comparable program) was 9.36 percent, a relative difference of 3 percent. Not bad at all!

While we're on the subject, let's talk about the retirement age. Why is it 65? Why not?

That age has been credited to — or blamed on — German Chancellor Otto von Bismarck. In truth, he didn't do it. The retirement age under Bismarck's social security system when it was established in the 1880's was 70. Before the passage of the Social Security Act in this country, 28 states and two territories has laws providing for payment of a pension (often no more than $1 a day) to the elderly, with the retirement age set at 65 or 70. (As an aside, let me mention that the first and most generous plan was in the territory of Alaska, which enacted its pension law in 1915, providing up to $35 a month to men age 65 and $45 a month for women age 60. But Alaska only had 446 people drawing pensions in December 1934.) The manner in which the federal government chose 65 as the minimum retirement age in 1935 was admittedly arbitrary and empirical.

Here's the empirical part. In 1934 we figured that men who were 65 years old could, on the average, expect to live another 12 years. For women it was 13 years. The bottom line was that we figured it would cost $22 billion in the aggregate to give a $25 monthly pension for life. And that was a lot of money in those days.

Now here's the arbitrary part. Age 65 was picked because 60 was too young and 70 was too old. So we split the difference.

I did the math. That was my role, and it was great on-the-job training. We started out with very primitive methods, and these were refined over the years. In a very basic sense, the Social Security Administration is still doing that sort of thing, only it's much more complicated, and it's done on a computer, which handles calculations that just couldn't be done a half century ago.

On November 4, my six weeks had run out, but the work of the committee, which was now less than a month away from its deadline, was far from over. In fact, more people were being brought in, and the operation was now four times the size that Witte had originally envisioned.

Witte's headaches also were building up. If he'd had enough hair, he might have been pulling it out. This was a big project with unrealistic deadlines, and the kind of people brought together to do the work, although experts in their fields, represented a peculiar kind of problem.

In his book *Development of the Social Security Act* [15], Witte wrote the following:

"Still more serious was the fact that nearly all of the specialists had their own ideas as to what should be done. No one was engaged who did not indicate a willingness to subordinate his own views to those of the committee and the President.

"Actually, however, this did not work out, and some of the principal members of the staff later on felt very hurt because their individual ideas were not adopted in toto.

"Another difficulty which developed was that the specialists employed set standards of perfection for their work which prevented completion of their reports in time so they could be of maximum use to the committee. Only a few of the major staff reports were completed by the time the committee had to reach its decisions."

That probably would not have made much difference anyhow. Witte said he didn't think members of the committee read what reports they did get very thoroughly.

Staff problems aside, the committee also had been saddled with a gaggle of advisory panels, and Witte said having all these people around was a mistake.

"The body was too large and too little time was allowed for its deliberations," Witte wrote of the Advisory Council. "The members of the council took their appointments by the President very seriously, and several had distinct objectives in mind."

None of them, however, were experts in the field of social insurance. They included clergymen, journalists, politicians, business and labor leaders, and more university types. Some of them got the impression that they were being used for window dressing. In the end this group delivered advice to the committee which was largely ignored.

The committee itself was having trouble, and the December 1 deadline came and went without a report being delivered to FDR. Finally a couple of days before Christmas, three members of the committee, Perkins, Hopkins, and Wallace, met for six hours in the chairwoman's home. Witte, Altmeyer, and Josephine Roche, an Assistant Secretary of the Treasury, also were present. It was termed an "unscheduled" meeting, and there were no minutes kept. It was from this secret session that the final report to the president, the foundation of the Social Security system, was shaped. (Sound familiar?)

The final report of the committee went to the President on January 15, 1935 [3]. It included the following recommendations:

Employment Assurance. Essentially, the nation owed a promise of work for every able-bodied individual. For the most part, jobs were to be generated by private enterprise. But where this fell short, and in times of economic hardship, the government should step in to provide public works jobs. "We regard work as preferable to other forms of relief where possible," the committee wrote.

Unemployment Compensation. This would be an insurance pool, financed by a payroll tax, run by the states and guided by the federal government. The committee saw this as a "front line of defense, especially valuable for those who are ordinarily steadily employed, but very beneficial also in maintaining purchasing power."

Old-age Security. The federal government would pay up to $15 a month per individual who was in need in the short run.   Over the long term, a system of earnings-related pensions would be financed by a tax shared equally by employee and employer.   The committee also recommended that the government get into the business of selling voluntary annuities that could be payable upon retirement. It admitted that the contributory program was incomplete because it did not address the retirement needs of the self-employed and certain professional groups.

Security for Children. The Depression had left many families destitute, and the states were unable to handle the burden.   Many of these families had no breadwinner and thus would not be helped by public works projects or unemployment compensation.   The committee recommended that the federal government offer aid to the states "for the protection and care of homeless, neglected, and delinquent children, and for child and maternal health services especially in rural areas."

Health. The committee flirted with the idea of national health insurance but said that it wasn't prepared to make a recommendation.   It asked for further study of the matter.

Roosevelt for the most part agreed with the committee's advice, but there was one part of the old-age pension system to which he flatly objected.   Under the financing scheme outlined by the committee, the Social Security program would be self-supporting for its first 30 years or so.   After that, as more people retired, the system would be under strain and would need money.   The committee suggested this come in the form of a government subsidy.

Under the committee's plan, the taxes on workers and employers together to support the system would rise over 20 years from 1 percent to 5 percent, but that wasn't going to be enough to keep the system afloat. Eventually the proposed government subsidy would have to cover about a third of Social Security's costs.

Even though this was something that wouldn't happen until around the mid-1960's, when the people responsible would have long been out of office or gone to their Great Reward, FDR didn't want to hand a mortgaged program to future generations. The President already was being stung by criticism for running budget deficits which were small in comparison with those we have had in the past decade, not only in dollar terms but also even relative to the federal expenditures. And he was a sharp politician who also was sensitive to the verdict that history would render on him.

FDR required that the program support itself through payroll taxes and whatever interest it was able to collect on money that built up in the trust fund.

So as the bill made its way from the committee in the Walker-Johnson Building to the White House to the Capitol, its work wasn't done. I still had a job, but there was no telling for how long. Congress was going to need technical help as it tried to write the legislation to put Social Security into effect, and we were the only ones in town who could provide it.

One thing that was missing from the administration's bill was a retirement test for the old-age benefits. There had been some discussion of giving a Social Security pension only to people who need it. That is a means test, an idea that has come up from time to time and is always rejected. But a retirement test is a sound idea. A retirement pension should only be paid to someone who's actually retired. The committee failed to provide a legal definition of that.

The bill still didn't have a retirement test even after the House passed it. The House knew that it needed one but couldn't come up with it. When the bill came out of the Senate, a very general provision was in the law, but not spelled out in detail, thinking that this would be worked out in regulations. The question then was what about a cost estimate for the final bill.

The two top actuaries who had been on loan to the committee had by this time gone back to their permanent jobs. This was the closest thing I had to a real job, so I was still there. Now some cost estimates were needed, and I was asked to do them. I was working under the direction of Murray Latimer, the chairman of the Railroad Retirement Board, who was serving as a technical adviser to the committee.

I would be the last person in the world to say that originally I figured out how to make these estimates, but having had the guidance to do it, then I understood how to do it. So when people would put variables in and say let's change the plan to do this or that or the other thing, I knew how to gear up the machine to do it.

I probably took my own work too seriously, as people do when numbers come out of a calculating machine or a computer. They seem to have a certain air of veracity and reality to them. However, I think I'll always realize that variation is possible.

At Roosevelt's insistence, the tax structure of the plan had been changed so that it would be self-supporting. Instead of increasing the combined employer-employee tax rate from 1 percent to 5 percent over 20 years, this rate would start out at 2 percent and rise much more rapidly to 6 percent.

The bill that passed the House was not self-supporting. It was going to build up a sizable fund, and it wasn't going to require a government subsidy in the valuation period, which was up to 1980. But the system obviously was not self-supporting because the fund balance was going to rise and then decrease. Something like under present law, as it happened. Under present law the best estimates currently are for the fund to increase until about 2025 and then go down to zero in 2036.

One of the things that was going to cause the fund to sink was that there was no retirement test. If what the House had passed became law, benefits were just going to start spewing out for everybody over age 65. Putting in the retirement test would cut the system's projected costs. The end result that we were shooting for was a system that would always be able to support itself, so I tinkered with the numbers until that's the way it came out. This wasn't really cooking the books, as I will explain later. Essentially we were moving numbers around until the system was shown as going into the black and staying there.

There was an element of these calculations that involved a fair amount of guesswork. Just because people *can* retire at age 65 doesn't mean that's when all of them *will* retire. Some people will keep on working.

In fact, people tended to do that then. There weren't a lot of savings, jobs were considered precious commodities, pensions were relatively rare and low, and there was no such thing as Social Security yet. If you stopped working at age 65, you stopped getting money, and that meant you could stop eating.

So I had to figure out, on the average, when people were going to retire. This was going to make a difference in what the system cost. The age that I picked was 67 1/2. The number looked reasonable. We knew that everybody wasn't going to retire at age 65. I also knew that they wouldn't all keep working until they were 75. The answer was somewhere in the middle. There was no real experience to go on, so I had to guess. Using age 67 1/2 the numbers worked out to show that the system stayed in the black and thus was self-supporting throughout the entire valuation period.

We were almost victims of our own success. The new estimates showed the Social Security fund building up to a peak in 1980 and leveling off there. The peak was the immense figure of $47 billion, which was an awful lot of money then. It was more than the national debt. And at that time this figure of $47 billion was widely discussed in the press.

(Interestingly, the balance in the Social Security trust funds reached $46 billion at the end of 1974 but then decreased during the remainder of the 1970's. At first glance, one might say that the actuarial estimates made in 1935, showing a $47 billion fund in 1980, were thereby shown to be great. But I would hasten to say that many counterbalancing elements occurred, such as program changes and inflation.)

This mammoth balance projected for 1980 and the public discussion of it has long been forgotten, but it became a hot issue at the time. People thought that with all that money lying around, it would just be too much of a temptation for the government. Some day we'd all wake up and the money would be gone, and the system as well as the government would be in debt.

It seems like a pretty arcane point, but there was a lot of popular criticism of this huge surplus then. There were even articles in Reader's Digest about it.

In the last few years, there's been a lot written about the Social Security system, and what gets me is when people write about what the original financing basis of the program was. I read something not too long ago by a fellow who said that the original financing provisions of the law set up a fully-funded insurance system, and then in 1939 they went to that "horrible" pay-as-you-go system.

Not true.

The fund under the 1935 Act was going to build up to $47 billion in 1980. That's not being fully funded, that's being self-supporting. Fully funded means that you could quit at any time, as an insurance company can, and still be financially sound. If all of an insurance company's policyholders quit paying premiums today, assuming that the insurance company had reasonably good investments, it could pay off all the claims that people had as of today.

But Social Security was not fully funded on that basis. If it had quit at any time, it never would have had enough money so that it could pay the accrued benefits. It is always assumed that there will be new entrants. And it did not change to a pay-as-you-go basis in 1939 because a sizeable fund was contemplated, although not as large as under the original law.

There were other myths about Social Security. One was that the program was designed to take people out of the labor market, and thus solve the Depression.

No way. It was established to provide a retirement floor of protection. It wasn't to take people out of the labor market because the original system was not going to pay any benefits until 1942, seven years later. And the benefits were going to average only about $17 a month. At the time people were earning about $100 a month on the average, so there wasn't a big incentive to retire on Social Security benefits.

Even with the 20/20 vision of hindsight, I think that the Committee on Economic Security did a good job. It seems to me that if it had had 10 times the amount of money and 10 times the amount of time, it could not have done much better.

There were limits on what could be done. There wasn't enough money to go around, but something had to be done at the time. We knew that as we went along through time, we'd develop a better plan. The main thing was to get started.

On June 30, 1935, the Committee on Economic Security folded up. The legislation was practically through, and the money to pay for running the committee was almost all gone. It had been a pretty good run. Instead of lasting 40 days, my job lasted 40 weeks.

There would probably be a job for me in the Social Security system, but it didn't exist yet. The bill establishing it would not pass Congress and be signed by the President until August 14, 1935.

For the time being, I was out of work.

CHAPTER FIVE

AN EPIDEMIC ERASED

In 1935, jobs in the rest of the country were hard to get. But this was Washington, so I got another job right away. I didn't even have to leave the building.

Hopkins' agency, the Federal Emergency Relief Administration, had been the landlord for the Committee on Economic Security. Now the agency had a new name: the Works Progress Administration, or WPA, and it was looking for a statistician. The job even came with a small raise.

I had decided that this job was going to be temporary, because I wanted to go back to work for Social Security. Few people knew better than I what a growth industry this was going to be. I had come up with the numbers. There were going to be billions of dollars spent on millions of beneficiaries. It was going to take thousands of people to carry this out.

In the summer of 1935 there was just one hitch in my grand plan.

Social Security didn't yet exist.

The act establishing the program was signed into law on August 14, 1935. There had been noisy opposition in the Senate, but the vote there was an overwhelming 77-6, supported even by some of the program's loudest enemies, including the loudest of them all, Huey Long of Louisiana.

But Long wasn't finished. Congress still had to appropriate the money to get the program operating, and this is where Long made his stand. He was choking off its money.

Arthur Altmeyer, who by this time had been confirmed as a member of the new Social Security Board, recalled watching the Kingfish try to take another bite out of the newborn agency.

"Senator Huey Long staged another filibuster on the closing day of the session while the last deficiency appropriation bill, which included the social security item, was still pending," Altmeyer wrote in *The Formative Years of Social Security* [6].

"I well remember watching the hands of the Senate clock move toward midnight, when Congress would adjourn *sine die*, and hoping against hope that the senator would end his filibuster which had no relation to social security. However, he was still talking when the presiding officer banged his gavel, signaling the end of the session," Altmeyer wrote.

We'll never know if Long had any other aces up his sleeve. If he did, he never got the chance to play them. He was assassinated on September 8, 1935 in a corridor of the Louisiana Capitol.

Meanwhile, the Social Security Board limped along with some money shuffled from the Department of Labor, and they started hiring a few people. I wasn't one of them. They didn't need actuaries yet. The first people aboard were the administrative types that you need to get an agency like that up and running. The real appropriation for Social Security wouldn't arrive until after Congress came back in 1936.

In the meantime, Congress had managed to pass the Railroad Retirement Act of 1935. This established a government pension system very much like Social Security, but as its name implies, it was for railroad employees only. It was passed and signed into law two weeks after the Social Security Act, and it had money to spend because people like Long didn't get in its way.

Nowadays it may seem anomalous to have a separate government retirement system for railroad workers. But back in 1935, railroad workers were a peculiar breed of cat, and they got special treatment. The nation was extremely dependent on the railroads at the time, and the unions representing these workers were very strong.

One of the benefits which the unions won for the workers was the inclusion in the system of two special features. The first was the crediting of service before 1937 for pension purposes, without requiring the workers to contribute. Second, the system took over almost the entire existing pension rolls of the railroad private pension plans.

From the workers' standpoint, those were the good points of the railroad private pension plans. The workers did not pay any contribution under that system. There was also a down side. The pensions had hardly any reserve funds, the minimum retirement age in some cases was as high as 70, and a worker could only be eligible after working for the railroad for many years and could only collect if employed at the time of reaching the retirement age.

As you can see, the old system had a lot of escape hatches in it for the employer. There was also one other problem. The Depression had taken its toll on some of the largest railroads in the country, and they were having trouble making their pension payments.

The workers were unhappy with their old pension system even when it worked, and now they came to the government asking for relief when their program was falling apart. Government obliged. Twice. The first attempt in 1934 was ruled unconstitutional and the 1935 rewrite of the law was headed the same way. But then FDR brought labor and management together and asked them to quit fighting over this. The railroads agreed to stop challenging it in court, and the unions agreed to some changes in the law to make life easier for the companies.

Through all of the court challenges, the Railroad Retirement Board had a staff and an actuarial office. I was approached about being essentially the No. 2 person on the board's actuarial staff, even though I wasn't yet a fully qualified actuary. (It took me until 1940 to pass all of the exams.) But I had more background than the other two or three fellows there, some of whom later did become fully qualified actuaries.

I left the WPA immediately and took this job in the fall of 1935. It was straight actuarial work. There was quite a lot of it because there was a lot of data around. The railroads had always been regulated, so there was an abundance of information on wages and ages of people, work history, and other things like that.

(The Board, by the way, has since moved its headquarters to Chicago, but in those early days it was headquartered in Washington.)

Jumping ahead for a moment, this experience with Railroad Retirement came in very handy later. In 1983-85, I was selected by railroad labor and management to be the chairman of the Railroad Unemployment Compensation Committee. I must have done a successful job in being neutral between the two groups, because in 1988 I was chosen as Chairman of the Commission on Railroad Retirement Reform, a *pro bono* job, for its two-year study (after having been named to the commission by House Speaker Jim Wright).

I still had my eye on the Social Security Board, as to when they'd really start up. And sometime about the summer of 1936, an appropriation was passed, the Social Security Board got money, and it really got organized. I was offered a job there and took it.

This was under unusual circumstances because there were

Civil Service rules and regulations that required things like exams. The Social Security Act originally permitted people to be hired without regard to Civil Service rules and regulations if they were "experts." It was through that loophole that the board hired W.R. Williamson as the Chief Actuary, which at the time was called Actuarial Consultant. He had been one of the two actuaries with the Committee on Economic Security, and he now left his job at The Travelers for good.

Williamson was genuinely an expert, and they paid him a lot of money. He was getting $8,000 a year, which was a fortune. In one way that was more than that job should have commanded. At the time the government pay scales were based rather loosely on how many people you had working for you. The actuarial staff at the Social Security Board was only going to be about 20 or 30 people, so in that sense his pay shouldn't have been that high.

But actuaries were rare, the board needed one, and it would have to pay top dollar.

There was no question about calling Williamson an expert, but there was a real debate over what to call Wilbur Cohen and me. We didn't look like experts. We were just a couple of pups in our early 20's. Besides, if they called us experts, they'd have to give us more money. The lowest paid expert got $3,200 a year, and the board only wanted to pay us $2,600 but didn't want to go through the hassle of the Civil Service system. Finally they swallowed hard, threw us the extra $600, and Wilbur and I were government experts.

I left the Railroad Retirement Board and started working for Social Security at the time they were building up an actuarial office there. Williamson hired a number of other people, both actuaries and technical people who specialized in insurance or pensions. One of them was a fellow named Birchard E. Wyatt, who later went on to become founder of what is now a very large actuarial consulting firm.

Williamson also hired Dorrance E. Bronson, an actuary from The Travelers, to be his top assistant and the second in command. I fit in as No. 3 in this pecking order.

Social Security was rapidly becoming a huge agency. At its height, the Committee on Economic Security had maybe 100 people working for it. Its offspring, Social Security, now had central administration, a records division, and field offices, employing more than 20,000 people. This was in the stone-age days before computers, when records were things made of paper kept in manila folders and filed away in drawers. It took an enormous number of people just to put the paper in the folders and put the folders in the drawers so they could be found again.

I came back to Social Security in October 1936 and hadn't been there a week before Cohen and I were dispatched on a mission. We were put on a train and sent to New York City, where we were to advise FDR's campaign committee on Social Security matters. Essentially, we were supposed to check facts and make sure that what the campaign was saying was factually correct.

As I recall, the order came from one of the members of the Social Security Board, all of whom, of course, had been appointed by FDR. Wilbur and I didn't take leave from our jobs. In fact, we were told to find a Social Security office when we got to New York and drop in. Our freight was being paid for by the Social Security Board, and this was to give our trip the cover of legitimacy. I don't remember if we ever got around to doing that.

We went to a hotel which had been taken over by the Roosevelt re-election campaign. Social Security was a hot item that fall of 1936, and Kansas Governor Alf Landon, the Republican presidential nominee, was doing everything he could to keep it that way.

Landon's ploy was more of a knee-jerk reaction. Nobody knew much of what the Social Security program was going to do.

Landon just made a big point that people were going to have money taken out of their checks starting the following year. He didn't talk about the benefits people were going to be getting down the road. He just hammered away at that one thought — someone is taking your money away from you, and that someone is named Roosevelt.

This was not one of the Republicans' prouder moments, as far as I was concerned. They engaged in scare tactics that were nothing short of shameful.

Altmeyer described this well:

"A week before the election the Industrial Division of the Republican National Committee flooded employers with millions of pamphlets, posters, and pay envelope inserts attacking the old age insurance system. The pay envelope inserts were headed, 'Notice — Deductions from Pay Start January 1,' and at the bottom were the following words in large black letters: 'Social Security Board, Washington, D.C.' This gave the appearance of an official notice. There was no mention of the benefits payable.

"The Hearst press ran front-page stories the day before the election attacking the old age insurance system. They were illustrated by a picture of a man stripped to the waist, wearing a chain with a dog-tag. It was captioned 'Snooping-Tagging' and carried this explanatory statement beneath: 'Each worker would be required to have one for the privilege of suffering a pay cut under the Social Security Act, which is branded as a 'cruel hoax'.''

There was indeed a cruel hoax going on, and it was against this backdrop that the Roosevelt campaign was making its defense of Social Security, the reason for sending Cohen and me to New York. (The dog-tag reference did have some basis in fact. The

Addressograph Corporation had made an offer to manufacture metal nameplates for everyone with a Social Security number. Altmeyer as chairman of the Social Security Board rejected the idea.)

I know that our trip seems like an open-and-shut case of political corruption, but things like this go on all the time. Maybe not as blatant as having a couple of government employees travel out of town at federal expense to help out with a presidential campaign.

Sometimes the line between right and wrong is very fine and hard to see. What if it didn't involve out-of-town travel? Suppose we had stayed in Washington, and the White House had sent over a list of questions to answer or statements to be examined for accuracy. Some lower-middle management government employee in his early 20's, as Wilbur and I both were, isn't going to ask a White House aide to take a saliva test to see if this request is political or on the level.

Occasionally we were asked to do more than just answer questions. Guys would bring speeches which they had written and ask us if they were correct. Later on, they would ask Wilbur and me to write those parts of the speeches ourselves when we found things that were all wrong.

We were only there a couple of days. It was an exciting thing to do, I thought. I don't know that anybody told us it was illegal but do it anyway. I wouldn't say that I did this because I wanted FDR to win. I did this because I wanted the ''facts'' to be facts.

I was sort of neutral on the issue of FDR and can't quite remember how I voted. I think that I probably voted for him because of the Social Security issue. I must confess that in later elections, I voted, and will continue to vote, for candidates solely on Social Security issues.

This was the one and only time that I helped in a campaign while I was a government employee, and it was the last presidential election where we could have gotten away with it. In 1939 Congress passed the Hatch Act, forbidding government employees from participating in political campaigns. It also protects them from pressure to assist a campaign or to contribute money to it.

At all other times my primary responsibility was making the cost estimates. I had been doing that for the plan as it went through Congress, and now it was my job to do these estimates for the proposals to change it that came up almost immediately. In fact, changing Social Security is one of the things about the program that has stayed the same through all these years. From the moment the program came into being, there has been fine tuning (and some not so fine) going on. People wanted to make it bigger, they wanted to make it smaller, they wanted it to cost less, they wanted it to bring in more money. This has been going on constantly.

A lot of this came from the 1937-38 Advisory Council, a blue-ribbon group of people from outside the agency. There's a picture of this first council sitting around a big table in their 1930's garb. Everyone looked stern. I was standing in the back of the room with the staff who churned out the memorandums when someone sitting at the table would pose a question. They'd say suppose we do this, suppose we take farmers in, suppose we increase benefits 10 percent with a minimum increase of $10? We worked out cost estimates and memorandums for things like that.

The recommendations of this council produced sweeping changes in the system in amendments that were passed in 1939. These gave benefits to wives and dependent children of retirees and to widows and dependent children of workers who had died. They also advanced the date of first availability of monthly benefits by two years, to January 1940, and increased benefits payable in the early years (and decreased those that would be payable several decades hence).

And of course when there's legislation, we'd get very busy because Congress doesn't just take what the Administration sends up. It modifies proposals and very frequently makes improvements. Although before 1939 I did not work directly with the congressional committees involved in Social Security legislation, still whatever information they wanted the Social Security Board prepared. Congress never had its own separate actuaries in this field. It has relied on the actuaries in the Social Security Administration.

In 1940, life seemed to stabilize. The Social Security system was chugging along. This was the year it started writing checks to retirees, and once that happened there was no turning back. It was here to stay.

So was I. Rudy and I then took the big step of buying a house in the Maryland suburbs, in an area where it wasn't unusual for stray cows to be wandering loose. The area has grown up considerably since then.

Living as far out of town as we did, we bought a second car, a wild extravagance that cost $60. It was an American Bantam, produced in Butler, Pa., and was a very interesting looking little car. It was just a tiny thing that held only two people. While it was good to have for going to the store, its real usefulness would come up in a couple of years when gasoline was being rationed. It was smaller than a lot of the cars on the road today, and it got great mileage. Maybe that's why the company didn't last. It was too far ahead of its time.

We became season ticket holders for the Washington Redskins. Season tickets then were something that they're not today: cheap and available. I think they cost something like $8 apiece. They were trying, to drum up business, so they kept their prices low, even by 1940's standards.

Anyway, it was at the old Griffith Stadium that we found ourselves on a Sunday afternoon, December 7, 1941. I couldn't tell you much about the game or even who was playing, but at some point the public address system started delivering emergency messages for people in the stands to go to their offices immediately. A lot of these people were generals and admirals. They never did say at the stadium that Pearl Harbor had been attacked. It wasn't until we got home and turned on the radio that we finally got the news. Newspapers put out extras on that Sunday evening.

Now that we were at war, the possibility of the draft arose. I had been in the ROTC at Lehigh because it had been required. You had to be in for two years. I was now wishing I had stayed in for four years because two years gave you nothing but a little knowledge of military science and tactics. If you stayed in four years, you got a commission. Anyhow, I was in just two years. I didn't like it.

It wasn't long in coming. My draft notice arrived after the first of the year. But another quirky event stepped into its path. I got an odd job offer from the Railroad Retirement Board, which by law has to have an actuarial valuation every three years.

That seemed straightforward enough, but the board's actuary, a fellow named Joseph Glenn (who had been my boss when I was at the Railroad Retirement Board in 1935 and 1936) had other ideas. He was a very strange and stubborn guy in some ways, but he was very capable. He had made the first actuarial valuation, and when it came time to do the second one, he just said "no." It was no use, he told them. It would show the same numbers as the first one.

Well, he was just all wrong on that. The law says do it, so you do it. So he quit. The board had some junior actuaries there who had not passed all their exams yet to be fully qualified. They were otherwise capable people, but they just weren't ready to fly solo. Due to all my past experience with the agency, the board asked me if I would make the valuation, and I agreed. This got me a draft deferment until the valuation was done.

By this time the board had moved its headquarters to Chicago, and taking this job meant I would have to leave Rudy at home. She was pregnant at the time with our first son, Jonathan, who would be born that October. I didn't like leaving her alone in that condition, but going to Chicago for the Railroad Retirement Board seemed at the time to be better for all concerned than having me put on an Army uniform and ship out for who knows where.

The valuation took several months, and in the meantime Jon was born. I returned home, and in May 1943, I got drafted. I had tried to get a direct commission in the Navy like a lot of actuaries and other professionals did. The doctors said my eyes weren't good enough for an officer in the Navy, but they were just fine for an enlisted man in the Army.

One more curve got thrown at the draft board. I was offered a job teaching math at the University of Rochester, a lot of it to military people because they were being sent back to school. The draft board didn't take too long to think that over before deciding it was no excuse.

So almost four score and one years after my grandfather donned a Confederate uniform, another Private Myers entered the service of his country. I went to Camp Lee, Va., for induction. On the various tests they gave, I did pretty well. They decided that I would do well in finance school because that involves mathematics.

I took basic training at Fort Benjamin Harrison, in Indiana. Of course at 30 years old, I was no longer a youngster. I guess I wasn't the world's best soldier. I could shoot a rifle well enough, but the marksman medal I got was the lowest one the Army gives. After I graduated from basic training, I was to go to an actual finance school and learn about how the Army keeps pay records.

But in the meantime, a friend of mine in Washington, Harold Dorn, a statistician who had been with the Public Health Service, was recruited and given a direct commission as a major. He was a bit older than I was, and had gone to work in the Office of the Surgeon General of the Army to handle their medical statistics. Mostly that involved collecting the statistics from all the different Army hospitals and medical posts, combining them and analyzing them. This friend began recruiting a staff. He thought reasonably well of actuaries and told me that he'd try to get me back to Washington if I was interested.

Quite naturally I was. In the meantime, when I was drafted, Rudy and the baby couldn't live alone in our home because we didn't have that much money. She took Jon and went to live with my folks (an experience all of them endured rather than enjoyed).

We rented the house out to a Navy officer. In fact, I had to pay off the delightful 4 1/2 percent mortgage because I couldn't meet the huge mortgage payments of $60 a month on the salary of a private. I had inherited a small amount of Baltimore and Ohio Railroad stock, and I had to sell it all. I probably did the wise thing in selling that stock because I suspect that it didn't amount to much over the years. Anyhow, we paid off the $5,000 due on the mortgage, and Rudy went to live in Elkins Park.

My friend, Major Dorn, decided to recruit some other statisticians, including actuaries. He knew two actuaries at Metropolitan Life, Ed Lew and Frank Weck, who were a bit older than I was. They could get direct commissions. He also contacted another actuary from the New York Life, Ed Williams, who had been drafted as I was and was still an enlisted man. He had us both brought back to Washington and got us direct commissions as second lieutenants.

Dorn said "I'd like you to get some experience at the grass roots. I'm going to get you assigned to Walter Reed Hospital while your commission is going through. Where the records start is from a hospital. And you work there for a few weeks, then you can come down to headquarters." So I worked at Walter Reed, and I lived in the barracks there. When I saw that everything was working out on a more or less permanent basis, I had Rudy come back to Washington. Fortunately the Navy officer who was here wanted to break the lease after three months or so. He was going to move, so the house was available. We had sold one of the cars to a neighbor, and he was neighborly enough to sell it back.

As long as I was assigned to Walter Reed, I had to stay there. The hospital is not too far from my house, but I couldn't sleep at home. That was against the rules. So I'd come home for dinner and go back to the barracks to sleep.

Well, after I'd been there three or four weeks and understood how the record system and statistics worked, I was brought downtown to headquarters in Washington. Still the commission hadn't come through. That took time. This posed a dilemma for the Army. They had a hard time figuring out how to get me from Walter Reed Hospital, where I was stationed, to downtown Washington, which was where I was supposed to be working.

Any sensible person would take one look at this problem and say: Walk out to the curb, wait for the bus, and ride it downtown to work. But this was the Army. So they made me the chauffeur for the Surgeon General, who also lived on the grounds at Walter Reed and went downtown to headquarters to work every day.

His regular chauffeur ended up just sitting around at Walter Reed while I was driving the car. He was really mad at me because he thought that I had taken his cushy job permanently, even though it would actually only be for a little while.

Life then was kind of hectic, almost like I was trying to play two roles in the same movie. I'd drive the general down to the office, and I'd go up to the office and work on statistics. If the general wanted to go somewhere, say, to the Pentagon, they'd give me a call, and I'd have to dash down to the garage, get the car and drive him over. Fortunately I'd been in Washington for some time and knew how to get around. I washed the car in the morning although washing a khaki colored car is an exercise in futility. It doesn't get that dirty. But the chauffeur had to wash the car every morning. It was a rule.

I got along well with Surgeon General Kirk. He knew that I was to do professional work at his office. But one night, he was taking the train to New York, and I drove him down to the station. After I carried his bag onto the sleeping car for him, he gave me a tip. A quarter. I thought this is a little unusual, being a professional actuary and all. Of course I didn't object. I just put it in my pocket and saluted.

This job only lasted a few weeks. When my commission finally came through, I was discharged as an enlisted man. That's the way the Army handles the paperwork of turning a private into a gentleman. You get a discharge and then you accept a commission as an officer. My discharge papers noted that I had acquired a specialty: chauffeur.

So with that behind me, I went to work full time on medical statistics and had a number of clerks working for me, compiling and consolidating these reports. Aside from my good-conduct citation, my biggest accomplishment was wiping out a typhoid epidemic. Yep. Just me, my pencil, and my squad of plucky clerks.

I was going through medical records of Army hospitals in the United States. There was one hospital, I noticed, where the summary for one year said there were 17 cases of typhoid fever. I thought that looked peculiar. Typhoid was pretty rare, especially in the United States. This record was from before I had come there. Previously the medical statistics division had been under the supervision of doctors. The fact that they were keeping statistics probably speaks volumes about their skills as men of medicine. And they weren't very good at keeping statistics either. That's why the Army had replaced them.

I found the hospital in question, traced down its records, and found the source of the typhoid epidemic. There had been 17 cases of respiratory illness that had been put on the wrong line of a form. A little work with an eraser and a pencil, and presto, the typhoid epidemic was gone.

I spent the rest of the war working on medical statistics. I didn't eapecially like being in the Army, but I liked doing what I was doing. Of course it beat the alternatives, such as being sent to some forsaken place to do finance reports or slogging through the mud somewhere. And it was great being at home. But I was getting awfully tired of that, and I wanted to get back to Social Security.

Sometime after V-E Day, in June 1945, I was approached by a friend who was working on the team that in essence was going to govern Germany. They wanted people in all fields including social security.

It sounded like interesting work, and besides, I thought it would get me out of the Army sooner. At the time, people were being discharged on the point system, and you got a lot more points for being in Germany than you did in the United States. I told him that I'd be glad to go, so I was given orders that separated me from the Office of Surgeon General. Then the Army told me to go home and stay there until I get further orders to go to Germany. I hung around the house for several weeks doing nothing but drawing pay. I waited and waited.

I didn't know it, but I was being lucky. The Army was doing its best to ship me out to Germany, but first it had to figure out if I was already there. There was another Robert J. Myers, a statistician, who was already in Germany hard at work in a field related to social security. So when the Army tried to cut the orders to send me to Germany, the people in Germany said, "You can't send him over here because he's already here."

They spent several weeks trying to figure this out. I was completely in the dark about it, so when the phone at home rang one day, I thought it might be the Army telling me to pack for Germany. It wasn't.

At the other end of the wire the man identified himself as Clarence E. Lea, the ranking Republican on the House Interstate and Foreign Commerce Committee. He said that the committee was considering Railroad Retirement legislation and would very much like my services. He asked if I'd be willing to work for him. This was an even better offer than Germany, so I said, sure, I'd be glad to, but I've got a little problem because I'm in the Army. Lea said that's no problem because he's in the Congress.

A week later I was out of the Army and working as a staffer for the House Interstate and Foreign Commerce Committee. I worked there for about four months and enjoyed it.

Rudy and I were able to celebrate V-J Day in Washington in August 1945. When the news was announced that the Japanese had surrendered, we, like a lot of other people in the area, went down to the White House just to stand outside and look. A big crowd had gathered to celebrate the end of the war.

Within two weeks, Rudy and I had another reason to celebrate, the birth of another son, Eric Laurence.

Once my work was done at the committee, I went back to the Social Security Administration in the spring of 1946. Just about that time, W.R. Williamson, my longtime boss, was having deep disagreements with his superiors.

Williamson began to think that the Social Security Act was all wrong, that it didn't do the right thing, that it paid some people too much, and that it didn't pay others enough. In fact, he was in favor of sort of a flat benefits system instead of the type of earnings-related graduated benefits system which we have.

I have an old book that belonged to him that had been published for the Committee on Economic Security. It gave a history of the committee and summaries of the research reports written by the staff. Unless you're really into this, it can be pretty dry reading. Williamson, though, filled the margins of many of the pages with his commentaries that sometimes were bitter and sarcastic.

I guess this just built up in him and affected his work. In the end, it was a combination — he was dissatisfied with the Social Security Board, and the Board was dissatisfied with him. In the meantime, Birchard Wyatt (who had founded his own actuarial consulting company), had died, and they needed somebody to hold the firm together. So in 1947 it was a good opportunity for Williamson, and he took it (Bronson had left to go with Wyatt sometime before I got back to Social Security in 1946.)

This meant that the original two top guys in my department were now gone. This left me as next in line, but the Board wasn't sure that making me the top actuary was such a good idea. I was just 35 years old, and although the Board had faith in me, the members knew it was important to have somebody in the position who was known and respected in the profession. The actuary is the guardian of Social Security's financial credibility.

Because the Social Security Administration had always been conscious that they wanted credibility of the actuarial estimates, they did not want to be accused of putting out low estimates so that proposed legislation to expand the program could be enacted. They wanted a truly independent, professional job done.

The Social Security Administration shopped the job around and looked for likely candidates. But they finally settled on me, and in 1947 I became the Actuarial Consultant (in 1965 the title was changed to Chief Actuary), the job I would hold until I left 23 years later.

By this time, Social Security was an institution. It came out of the Depression, survived the war and outlived its founder, Franklin D. Roosevelt.

I was still in the Army when FDR died in April 1945. Even though I was a Republican, I liked him because of what he'd done for Social Security. When Harry Truman took office, I wasn't worried about Social Security. For one thing, Truman was a supporter of the program, and for another it was too big for him to destroy.

I was convinced that Social Security was here to stay, that it was working well, and had broad support. This was no accident. FDR had once said that he was going to finance Social Security in such a manner that "no damned politician" was going to destroy it. It was just set up so well, so that once it got started and it was operating, it no longer depended on any one person being there to support it. Once the system started, I don't recall FDR as being that prominent in pushing for changes. His mind was probably more occupied with the situation in Europe and throughout the world. The point is that it didn't even need him to decide when changes were necessary. The momentum for that could now come from elsewhere, from the Social Security Board, from labor, and from management.

The question from here on was not whether there would be a Social Security system, but rather how big it would be and what it would do.

There were always people who wanted to expand the program, such as greatly increasing the benefit level or adding national health insurance. I called many of its strongest supporters "expansionists." Personally, I think very, very highly of Social Security, but I'm not in favor of Social Security doing the entire job of economic security for the people of our country.

This is where the struggle would be, and really remains to this day.

CHAPTER SIX

CITY ON THE HILL

Anyone who comes to Washington should spend some time just sitting in the galleries of Congress to watch the members come and go. There are men and women, black and white, fat and thin. Some are serious, some are buffoons. There are scoundrels and scholars.

They are, in other words, pretty much like the rest of us.

Congress is a big, sometimes slow-moving institution that's easy to ridicule and criticize. Much of it is theater, and often the acting can be pretty bad. Maybe we expect too much of our leaders. Maybe that's why there are only four faces on Mount Rushmore.

Congress gets its share of the blame for the financial mess that the nation is in. It takes political courage to say no, and that is often a commodity in short supply. So money gets spent, often money we don't have, and the country is in a hole.

I'm proud to say that's not the case with Social Security. The system is robust. In this last decade of the century, it is taking in far more money than it is spending. As we have seen, there have been times when it has gotten out of kilter, but those times have been rare because they've been the exception, not the rule.

The rule has been that Social Security must always be kept financially solid. It's a system built on a promise, and if that promise isn't kept, there's nothing left. Congress deserves the credit for this. In the last half century, members of the House and Senate have acted responsibly and seriously in maintaining and improving the Social Security system.

There are wide differences of opinion in Congress over what that system ought to be, how much it ought to cost, to what extent it should protect our citizens, and to what extent they must take the responsibility for protecting themselves. But since the Social Security Act became law in 1935, its foes have gone away or changed their minds. The system really has no enemies in Congress anymore — or at least they keep mighty quiet. It is more in danger from the harm that could be done by people who mean well.

Just as our nation has changed since 1935, so the Social Security system has changed. The tinkering, adjusting, and inventing has been almost constant and began even before the program issued its first monthly benefit check.

For more than two decades, I had a unique association with Congress as this work went on. In fact, I labored so closely with the House Ways and Means Committee that the relationship may have violated the spirit, if not the letter, of the constitutional doctrine of separation of powers. I later did the same to a somewhat smaller degree with the Senate Finance Committee.

This relationship caught the attention of political scientist John F. Manley, who wrote about it in his book about this influential House committee, *The Politics of Finance* [11]:

"Ways and Means worked so closely with some executive department employees that Robert J. Myers, the Social Security Administration's head actuary, is identified on some Committee publications as 'Actuary to the Committee.' Myers, a professional technician, works in a confidential relationship with the Committee and is expected, by everyone concerned, to supply honest cost estimates on social security legislation regardless of how it may affect the Department's case."

My work as the actuary to the Ways and Means Committee is something that developed in 1949. The government was a different place then, Congress particularly. The Congress didn't have the big staff that is has now in the committees. When the committees took up legislation they tended to borrow people. Now the committees bulge with full-time staffs. But in those days, people were brought in temporarily from a variety of places, from the Library of Congress for example, to do some work and then went back to their regular jobs when they were done.

One reason for this practice, at least in the beginning, was that actuaries were still relatively scarce. If the congressional committees had gone off to recruit an actuary, they'd have had trouble finding anybody, let alone somebody who had any experience.

In a way, I think that the way things were done in those days was better. It was practical and efficient. Now much of the development of legislation seems to come from the staff and is presented to the members as something of a finished package. It used to be the other way around. Members of Congress used to develop the legislation and give it to a small staff to make certain the i's were dotted and the t's were crossed.

To my knowledge, no one ever questioned the propriety of my serving in this capacity. People could rightfully say that my role violated the separation of powers. I was, after all, an employee of the government's executive branch. Given the mutual suspicion that has grown up between Congress and the Presidency in the last two decades, an arrangement such as this is probably out of the question now. However, in the Social Security actuarial field, and to a somewhat lesser extent with Medicare, the congressional committees still rely on actuaries from the Social Security Administration and the Health Care Financing Administration for cost estimates.

I don't know if there was anything in writing about my being loaned out to Congress, but it was a rather formal arrangement. The committee chairman would call up Altmeyer or whoever the commissioner was, and that would be it. My work was confidential. I didn't tell the committee what was going on at the Social Security Administration, or the other way around, and this was the understanding of how things would be.

Beginning in 1950, Congress took up Social Security legislation every couple of years. From time to time, these amendments to the Social Security Act involved major expansions of the program. Often they included a boost in the benefits, and it was pure coincidence that fatter checks went out in election years.

My job during this time was twofold. First, we had to keep track of the financial health of the system and spell it out in the annual Trustees Reports. The second part involved examining changes proposed to round out the program. In some cases these changes were ideas from within the agency itself, where the policymakers were very active at trying to expand the program.

Some of these changes I thought desirable. As to others, I wasn't in favor of that much expansion. But we always had to figure out how much these changes would cost and how to pay for them, often through a combination of raising the earnings base and boosting payroll tax rates. Any long-range surpluses which had developed were also recognized.

There was no legal requirement that anybody do this, but in practice the House Ways and Means Committee and the Senate Finance Committee had such a rule. They wanted to keep Social Security soundly, actuarially financed on a long-range basis.

I don't want to sound immodest, but I suppose if one were to trace the history of this requirement, it would lead to me. In doing my estimates, I would always look at the long-term effects of a proposal. Then if into the distant future its costs and revenues were in line with each other, I would pronounce the system actuarially sound as it would be affected by the proposal at hand.

This approach was strongly supported by House Ways and Means Chairman Wilbur Mills, and the other members of the committee generally went along. They took the view that the long-range had to be considered, and that you couldn't just make certain there would be enough money to let the program limp along until the next election.

So these estimates showing the long-range balance sort of became a control. It grew into a traditional practice for Congress to follow and was an informal rule that the House and Senate committees lived by. Every time a committee would approve some sort of change in the program, the panel's report would conclude by saying that, with all the changes that were being proposed, the system is still actuarially sound.

My office was just at the foot of Capitol Hill in a building that has since been named after Wilbur Cohen. Only part of the actuary's staff was in that building, however. The people doing the short-range work were in Baltimore, and the people doing the long-range work were in Washington. These two groups were combined and placed under my supervision in 1965, and there was talk of moving the whole operation to Baltimore. I resisted it. As things stood, I would not have to go to Baltimore very often because the people doing the short-range work did an excellent job and, quite frankly, they rarely needed me. But I wanted to stay in Washington to be near the Capitol.

Occasionally the organizational freaks in the Social Security Administration would increase the pressure to make the move. It made sense to them to have the actuary's operation under one roof. I had to go running off to Wilbur Mills once to put a stop to this, and Mills carried the ball for me. I could always talk to Cohen, and we did discuss this. I guess I went behind his back in talking to Mills, but I thought that Cohen needed a little more persuading, and Mills could do it. My office stayed in Washington.

I believe that just my being there when these bills went through had an effect on Congress. A person is easier to ignore if he's nothing but a name at the bottom of a piece of paper. My going up to the Hill year after year made me more real to them than a faceless bureaucrat whom they could dismiss. Out of sight, out of mind, even if only 40 miles away.

My relationship was much closer to the House Ways and Means Committee during these years than to the Senate Finance Committee. This is because the bills would originate in the House, where the Ways and Means Committee has great power. So that's where most of the work had to be done. Invariably, as with tax legislation, the House as a whole operated on a closed-rule basis, under which it could accept or reject the Ways and Means bill but could not make changes at random. Occasionally, a vote would be permitted on one important feature in a bill, such as whether to increase the retirement age.

By the time the bill got to the Senate, it already had been pretty well developed. Nonetheless, the Senate Finance Committee always made some changes in the House bill. Although the Senate as a whole can change the bill, they don't usually do so from what the Finance Committee reports out.

I was never paid by the Ways and Means Committee nor the Finance Committee, nor did the committees ever reimburse the Social Security Administration for my services. But on one occasion when I was on loan to Senate Finance, that committee did ask Altmeyer if it could pay for my services. Arthur told them not to bother. He was a diplomat and politically astute. The committee was grateful to the Social Security Administration for lending expert help, and Altmeyer was grateful that the expert was his.

The Ways and Means Committee would work from a laundry list of proposed changes. The members would pick and choose, dropping some items from the list and adding others. Finally, they would come up with a list of desirable changes which they'd want to make in the program, and they would ask what it would cost.

Frequently I would be able to prepare some of my studies ahead of time because I had a pretty good idea of some of the questions I was going to be asked. What I wanted to avoid was going into the committee room, have somebody pop a question on me, and be unable to deliver some kind of answer. I didn't want to have to tell the committee that I'd get back to them in a couple of days or a couple of weeks. When the committee's moving, it's like a train rolling down the tracks, and you've got to have your baggage aboard.

Sometimes, because I'd been doing this for so long, I was able to make the calculations off the top of my head. On occasion, I'd take a flying guess, particularly if it was a little item. For example, if I were asked about the cost of paying survivor benefits to dependent grandchildren of workers — that is, children being supported by their grandparents because both of their parents are dead or disabled — I could reply almost immediately that the cost would be negligible.

I knew the figures well enough so that when asked a question like that, I'd stare off into space toward a distant corner where the walls would meet the high ceiling of the committee room. That became sort of a long-standing joke with some people. If I made a mistake, I would go back later and revise it, but these were things that you could do with reasonable accuracy.

One of the forces in play in the 1950's and 1960's that no longer operated after 1972 was the fact that Social Security had, in essence, a built-in money machine. The actuarial estimates were made using static economic conditions, assuming that wages wouldn't rise and prices wouldn't change. While no economist can predict with certainty what the economy will do, there is one thing that all of us know that it *won't* do: it won't stand still. But this was the assumption on which our numbers were based from 1935 to 1972. The Social Security system came to recognize inflation in an institutional sense in 1972, when expansion of the earnings base and increases in benefits were automatically tied to it.

I didn't do things the old way because I didn't believe that inflation would inevitably occur. I knew it would be there, and it always has been. But *not* taking it into consideration kept the system on absolutely solid ground. Until the automatic cost-of-living adjustments were written into the law, benefits would stand still — inflation or no inflation — until an act of Congress moved them.

Trying to guess what Congress would do about benefits in the future to deal with inflation would be just that: a guess. Benefits could, of course, be expected to go up, but nobody could know by how much.

My argument was that as long as benefits were standing still, so would everything else, at least as far as our assumptions were concerned. Nevertheless, there was some pressure from economists on the Social Security Administration staff to do otherwise and take inflation into account. The rationale was that it was a simple recognition of reality, and that it ought to be reflected in the estimates.

I would acknowledge reality, of course. Wages and productivity could be expected to go up over time. But the benefit structure and the financing provisions are static, and the program is built around that. I said that, as conditions changed, we could recognize that, increase benefits, and keep them up to date. But to anticipate these in advance is deceptive because in essence you're counting your chickens before they hatch. I always believed that part of the pressure for me to use dynamic economic conditions was to make the program appear to cost less than it otherwise would, so that the expansionists could get their way.

It's a little complicated, but here's how it would work. If wages rise, you take in more money. But the benefits which you pay out don't rise as rapidly. The reason for that is because the formula for computing benefits is weighted to pay proportionally more on lower earnings than on higher earnings. So while benefits go up as earnings rise, it's not on a one-for-one basis.

If all of this is factored in without Congress giving some sort of cost-of-living raise in the benefits, it looks as if the program costs less than it really does. That's because the spending, as measured by percentage of payroll, goes down.

Here is where human nature takes over, because if that result happens, there will be political pressure to liberalize the program, leading to the financial hazard of over-expansion.

I'd explain this to the economists, and they'd tell me to forget about it. But that's not the honest, or the proper, or the fair way to do it. If I had been ordered to do this, I would have refused and resigned. The argument never escalated to that, however.

So doing things my way was not only financially safe, it even generated money. As wages went up and benefits did not, the system began to show a surplus over the long run. Not a big surplus, but it was there, and it could be used for whatever you wanted, whether for increased benefits or to expand the program.

Every couple of years, usually taking effect just before an election, the benefits were increased by an arbitrary percentage that usually bore some relation to the changes in the Consumer Price Index and also to the money available. These changes were not directly related to the CPI, but were just sort of bargained. Some people would say let's give 8 percent, some would say let's give 5 percent. Maybe they'd settle on 6 percent or 7 percent, and often the House would say one thing and the Senate something else.

At the same time, these proposals would increase the maximum taxable earnings base, in part to recognize inflation in wages and in part to provide additional income to finance the benefit increase. Although in one sense the benefit increase was arbitrary, it was controlled by how much financing was available, or would be made available by changes in tax rates, earnings base, or expansion of coverage to more employment groups.

So did either the Senate Finance Committee or the House Ways and Means Committee ever approve a Social Security bill that I thought was wrong? When you say wrong, there might have been things in there that I didn't like, but when I looked at it just from the standpoint of financing, the bills were almost always adequately financed.

In the final analysis, when Ways and Means would come to the end of the markup on a bill and get the package together, Mills would ask me, "Bob, is this package that we've now developed actuarially sound?" And I could tell him that it was because during all of the discussions that had led up to that point, the financing had been revised to keep up with the changes that were being made in the benefits. They never planned to pay out a dollar without figuring out where it was going to come from.

In determining actuarial soundness in the 1950's and early 1960's, the system was projected off into perpetuity. Then in 1965 it was changed to the next 75 years because the Advisory Council thought that it ought to be changed. In financial terms, the difference is slight, and the change was mostly for cosmetic purposes. The reason for the action of the Advisory Council was that forever is infinite, and infinity is an intellectually confusing idea.

In actuarial terms, there's not much difference between 75 years and forever. Suppose you lend $100 at 3 percent interest, and somebody agrees to pay you $3 a year forever. That's an infinite amount of money, but it has a finite value. So you can get finite present values of an infinite series. In essence, you make the cost estimates for about 75 years ahead — and this is all on static economic assumptions — and then you assume by that time everything levels off. The costs rise and then plateau at 75 years. It's a certainty that costs are not going to level off at 50 or 60 years. You can, therefore, make an actuarial valuation that really extends out into perpetuity.

There were people who said we ought to make our projections only for the next 10 or 15 years. That one really got my back up. It wasn't a battle with the higher-ups; it was pretty much within the staff. The trouble with that, I always said, is that we know from a population standpoint what is going to happen for the next 75 years or so. Everybody who is going to be over 65 years old in the next 65 years is already born. And we know for certain there's going to be a rising trend in the aged population for quite a while. If we just stop at 10 or 15 years, we're not putting forth the whole truth.

Although you do know reasonably well the size of the retired population, the one variable is the size of the working population. You don't know that. The people who are going to be 30 years old in 50 years won't be born for another 20 years.

Even in dealing with the known population, there is some softness to the numbers because there are assumptions you have to make about mortality in the future. In general, mortality is going to improve, and people are going to live longer. That's always been the case, at least in the world before AIDS. Although I don't think the spread of the acquired immune deficiency syndrome will have a significant effect on overall mortality in the future, it does hold that potential. There are people who argue that matter both ways. The general view is that it will be contained as people know more about it, and maybe there will be some sort of a cure, or at least a treatment, for it.

Operating a system like this is like navigating a ship across the ocean heading for a particular port. When you leave the dock, you point the boat where you intend to go. But unpredicted storms come up that blow your ship this way and that. Then you figure out where you are, you look at the map and the stars, and you turn the wheel accordingly to head for the intended port. In this analogy, an actuary is like a navigator.

A lot of what the committees did was guided by the actuarial estimates. If a proposal cost too much, they wouldn't do it. I'm sure that many of them, for instance, had soft spots in their hearts for widows and would like to have done more, but there was the question of cost.

This put a very heavy responsibility on me, and I would try to give the very best cost estimates whether I liked the change or not, or whether I knew the Social Security Administration liked the change or not.

After weighing the costs and the benefits, though, Congress did summon the will to change the system. Some of the principal changes are summarized in the following paragraphs:

1939 Amendments. Before the first monthly benefit check ever went out, Congress drastically altered the character of the system by adding benefits for family members and survivors, including a retired worker's wife at least 65 years old or with children under age 18 (and such children too), a surviving widow aged 65 or over, a surviving dependent parent aged 65 or over, surviving children under age 18, and the mother of those children. Under the original Social Security Act, benefits could be paid only to retired workers who were at least 65 years old.

The 1939 act also extended coverage to workers over age 65 who were in covered employment. The original 1935 act had restricted this to workers under 65 years old.

1950 Amendments. Work on this started in 1949 and was really the first major change in Social Security since before World War II. Because there was no provision in the law for automatic raises to keep up with inflation, benefits were way out of line, so the raise that took effect in September 1950 boosted the checks by 77 percent. This sounds like a lot (and in fact was the largest single increase in Social Security's history), but it was the first raise since January 1940, when the first monthly benefits checks were mailed out. In the meantime, inflation, as measured by the Consumer Price Index, had gone up by 75.5 percent, so once the raise took effect, the buying power of the benefits had gone up by just 0.9 percent relatively. This year also marked the extension of coverage to almost all public employees, except those already covered by a government retirement system, and to many self-employed persons, farm and domestic workers, and employees of charitable, educational and religious organizations. The 1950 amendments also extended Social Security's reach beyond the 48 states, District of Columbia, Hawaii, and Alaska to include

Puerto Rico, the Virgin Islands, and Americans working abroad for U.S. employers.

1952 and 1954 Amendments. Benefits in 1952 went up 15 percent, again beginning with the September checks, which was 5.2 percent higher than the rate of inflation since the last raise. By coincidence, the checks were received in early October, just a month before the election. Two years later, the benefits rose 13 percent, while inflation in the meantime had been just 0.5 percent, giving an effective boost in buying power of 12.4 percent. In 1954 coverage again was extended by including self-employed farmers and employees of state and local governments under retirement systems who chose to participate. This meant that virtually all workers in the country either were covered or had the option to be covered by Social Security. Similar *ad hoc* benefit increases were made in 1959, 1965, 1968, 1970, 1971, 1972, and 1974. Some of these were more than was justified by the increases in the CPI (especially the one in September 1972).

1956 Amendments. Social Security benefits were extended to the disabled, not just the retired, the widowed, and the orphaned, but there were rather substantial limitations. These benefits applied to workers between the ages of 50 and 64 who were totally and permanently disabled. It also provided benefits to children of retired and deceased workers at least 18 years old who were totally and permanently disabled before age 22.

The minimum retirement age for women was reduced to 62, although benefits for taking this early retirement were lower than if the worker retired at age 65. The reduction was actuarially neutral, meaning that on the average a worker could expect, taking into account the time value of money, to collect the same total amount of benefits over the course of a lifetime, regardless of whether retirement was taken at 62 or 65 or in between. In 1961, men were given equal treatment with women as to the possibility of taking actuarially reduced benefits at ages 62 to 64.

1965 Amendments. This was a rough year for the American Medical Association. Two things that organized medicine mightily opposed were passed into law anyway. The first was Medicare, providing health insurance for the nation's elderly. Doctors saw this as socialized medicine, a notion that makes their blood run cold. The other major defeat for doctors was extension of Social Security coverage to include self-employed physicians. Restrictions on disability benefits were relaxed to include long-term, not just permanent, disability.

1972 Amendments. Beginning in 1975, automatic adjustments to benefits were tied to the rise in the Consumer Price Index.

1977 Amendments. At attempt was made to correct problems with the procedures for automatic adjustment of benefits, and in the process other mistakes were made. One nearly bankrupted the system, and the other created the "notch babies." In 1977 I no longer was Chief Actuary of the Social Security Administration, but I was working as a consultant to the Republicans on the Senate Finance Committee. Their views did not prevail, and this was the year that broke the standard requiring the long-range actuarial soundness of a Social Security bill. The majority view was to let the future take care of itself. As we have seen, the results of that were nearly disastrous.

1983 Amendments. The system was saved from collapse, but the "notch" problem remained unresolved (and really no way existed to solve it in a reasonable, equitable manner).

With one exception, my relations with Congress after 1983 consisted of occasional contacts with congressional staffers on various technical matters and formal testimonies before various committees, usually by invitation. I've testified on various subjects such as the retirement earnings test, the treatment of women under Social Security, the notch-baby problem, extension of Medicare to beneficiaries aged 62-64, making the Social Security Administration an independent agency, and changing the financing basis to pay-as-you-go. During my career, I've testified around 150 times. It's always been a thrill and something I've enjoyed.

On one occasion I had a different role. In mid-1986 the legislative session was drawing to a close, and several Social Security matters were still pending. My long-time friend, Pete Singleton, the Ways and Means Minority Chief of Staff, lost his Social Security counsel. He could not get a replacement on loan from the Social Security Administration or elsewhere. I offered to pinch hit and was accepted.

So I got a "permanent" congressional appointment, although the intention (and the actuality) was to stay only until the legislative session ended. As with my 1981-83 employment by the Social Security Administration and the National Commission on Social Security Reform, the pay was low (because of the deduction of my Civil Service Retirement pension), but the pleasure was great.

The high point of this, my last federal job, was being on the floor of the House when a bill making the Social Security Administration into an independent agency — which I strongly favored — passed by a vote of 401-0. However, the Senate never acted on the bill and it died at the end of the session.

Through all of these years, it has been a privilege and an honor to have worked with Congress. As an institution, it can take great pride in preserving and enhancing the program. Special mention is due, I think, to a handful of its members.

The following House members left lasting impressions with me:

Robert ("Muley") Doughton, D-North Carolina. He was Chairman of the Ways and Means Committee when I became Chief Actuary in 1947. But Doughton was born when North Carolina was still part of the Confederacy, and was in his mid-80's. He was slipping, and the real powers behind the throne at Ways and Means were Mills and Jere Cooper. Doughton was a very fine gentleman. He just didn't really have possession of all the facts and wasn't that interested in the details of the Social Security program.

Jere Cooper, D-Tennessee. Cooper, who followed Doughton, was a quite capable guy, but he was no Mills (who is discussed at length at the end of this chapter). He examined matters thoroughly and had a firm understanding of matters relating to Social Security and taxation.

Al Ullman, D-Oregon. He was a very good Ways and Means chairman and tried to understand all aspects of pending legislation. He was a hard-working, capable, knowledgeable guy, but he didn't wield the power that his predecessor, Mills, had. Part of that was due to the post-Watergate reforms that diluted the power of the committee chairman and gave it to chairmen of the subcommittees.

Dan Rostenkowski, D-Illinois. As chairman of the Ways and Means Committee, he's autocratic, even more so than Mills was. He's a strong advocate of protecting Social Security into the distant future by requiring actuarial soundness over 75 years. He has a large and very capable staff on the Subcommittee on Social Security. With the subcommittee system, he doesn't have the need to be as well informed on Social Security as was the case before this system. But at least during the 1983 amendments, Ways and Means bypassed the subcommittee system and went straight to the full committee because it was an emergency, and there just wasn't time to do otherwise.

Jake Pickle, D-Texas. As Chairman of the Ways and Means Subcommittee on Social Security for many years (now, Chairman of the Oversight Committee), he had a deep, searching interest in all aspects of Social Security. His independence of thinking was exemplified by his realization during the crisis years of the early 1980's that a substantial part of the solution to the program's long-range problems was to increase the retirement age. He saw that this was logical in light of increasing life expectancy in the past and its likely continuation in the future. He took this bold step — and took many fellow Democrats with him — in spite of the strong opposition of the House Democratic leadership and the indomitable Claude Pepper.

Andy Jacobs, D-Indiana. Currently he is Chairman of the Subcommittee on Social Security of Ways and Means. He's a real character. He's a thinker, and he follows his own drummer. As far as I'm concerned, guys like that are fine, even when they disagree with me (which he sometimes does and sometimes does not).

Philip Burton, D-California. I saw Mills take him down a couple of pegs once on the House floor. The issue and the other particulars are a bit hazy and really are unimportant. What I do remember is the good feeling I had when I saw Mills lower the boom on this guy. I just didn't like the way Burton behaved or the language he used. I had a friend at the Social Security Administration who had to have dealings with Burton. A lot of this was on the phone, and the practice at the time was to have a secretary listen in on the conversation and take notes. There wasn't anything sinister in that. It was just to have someone taking notes to make sure, for example, that requests were filled. But when Burton called, this friend would tell his secretary to just hang up the phone so that she wouldn't have to listen to that foul mouth. I had very little to do with Burton. He's the only man in Congress whom I didn't like. I don't think Will Rogers ever met him, either.

Claude Pepper, D-Florida. Personally, I quite admired him for all the zip and steam he had at his age. I liked him, even though our views often were at odds. However, I deplored the fact that he really didn't know much about the subjects and didn't think much about them. He depended mostly on his staff. As Chairman of the House Select Committee on Aging, he was the reigning advocate of the elderly. Anything that was for the elderly, he was for, but they weren't things that he necessarily thought up himself. However, on the other hand, you've got to give him credit. When the agreement was reached by the National Commission on Social Security Reform, of which he was a member, he went along with it even though he didn't like some of the things which the commission did. He had given his word, and he stuck to it. On one matter in 1983, the House did have a choice: raising the retirement age or raising taxes. True to form, Pepper was against raising the retirement age and was for raising the eventual tax rates. But once he lost on that point, he didn't go around making speeches against the reforms. He kept his eye on the larger issue of saving Social Security from collapse.

John Byrnes, R-Wisconsin. For many years he worked closely with Mills as the ranking Republican on the Ways and Means Committee. He was hard-working and bright, and he made a real effort to understand what was going on. There are many members of Congress who don't do that. He was in the same league with Mills.

George Bush, R-Texas. His was one of the rare appointments of a freshman congressman to the Ways and Means Committee. He came to the meetings dealing with Social Security and tried very hard to understand the issues. However, perhaps understandably, he never took the lead on Social Security.

Barber Conable, R-New York. A real intellect. He didn't react to matters just because they were liberal or conservative. He could read and think, and he did both.

He took Byrnes' place as the ranking Republican, and he served on the National Commission on Social Security Reform as one of the primary movers to obtain the successful consensus package.

Willis Gradison, Jr., R-Ohio. He had worked at HEW and knew something about the subject of Social Security. He has a good mind and doesn't make it up before he hears the discussion.

Bill Archer, R-Texas. He's quite conservative and is not a great Social Security enthusiast. But he was quite deeply concerned about the program and was very conscientious about his responsibilities, especially when he was a member of the National Commission on Social Security Reform. His views didn't always agree with mine, but when I gave him advice, he would listen.

Similarly, various senators require some special mention, including the following:

Harry Byrd, D-Virginia. He was Chairman of the Senate Finance Committee. My relations with him were always cordial. He wasn't as knowledgeable as Mills, and he relied more on his staff. He was quite a gentleman and was very nice to people, but he often just didn't care to understand what was going on.

Robert Kerr, D-Oklahoma. He was a very smart guy, but I don't know that he worked at it that hard. He asked good questions and could understand the answers.

Russell Long, D-Louisiana. The son of Huey Long and another genuine character. He was bright, but he didn't always apply himself to the issue of Social Security. Long was Chairman of the Senate Finance Committee, but unfortunately he wasn't too impressed with demanding that Social Security remain actuarially sound over the 75-year valuation period. (Now it's written into the law that you can't make changes that have more than a negligible effect over five years in terms of dollars, and over 75 years in terms of percentage of payroll unless certain special procedures are followed (such as super-majority votes, rather than simple majorities). This is called the "firewall." In my view, the 75-year firewall is a great idea, but there is no necessity for the five-year one. After all, wouldn't it make sense if an increased cost for the first five years produced a much larger savings over the long run? And yet such a proposal would fail the "firewall" test. Actually the five-year firewall is desired by the budgeteers, even though Social Security is ostensibly removed from the general budget.)

Bob Dole, R-Kansas. One of the quickest and brightest minds in Congress. You could tell him something once, and he would absorb it and be able to speak on the subject with such authority that you'd think he'd known about it all his life. As chairman of the Senate Finance Committee in the early 1980's and as a member of the National Commission on Social Security Reform, he was intimately familiar with the problems of the Social Security system and is one of the individuals responsible for saving it in 1983.

Carl Curtis, R-Nebraska. A conservative Republican who served both in the House and Senate. I knew him when he was a member of the Ways and Means Committee. He was not in favor of expanding Social Security, and in fact he did support cutting it back here and there. He and Altmeyer tangled bitterly in the 1950's, and I know that Arthur saw him as an enemy of social insurance. Curtis believed deeply that the system ought to deal fairly with everybody. I advised him in the early 1970's, although I sometimes disagreed with him.

John Heinz, R-Pennsylvania. A moderate Republican whose untimely death in an airplane accident in 1991 was a significant loss to Social Security. He served on the National Commission on Social Security Reform and had great interest in not using Social Security for general-budget purposes. As a very wealthy man, he was neither in favor of "giving away the store" to those less fortunate without regard to the financial feasibility of the proposal, nor did he think that everybody should be able to take care of themselves completely.

Bill Armstrong, R-Colorado. Another conservative and another member of the National Commission on Social Security Reform. He was actively interested in Social Security and was willing to listen to opposing views. There were no members of Congress whom I would classify as enemies of Social Security intent on its destruction. But I would classify some of them the same way as I do Ronald Reagan: they didn't personally like Social Security, and if they had a choice in the matter, the program wouldn't exist. However, they recognize the practicality of it. They know their constituents want it, so they work for a system which they believe is sound. Curtis, Armstrong, and Archer are in this category.

Daniel Patrick Moynihan, D-New York. I've known Pat for some time. I worked with him on the National Commission on Social Security Reform and have been associated even more closely with him in recent years (as I will discuss in the final chapter). Pat worked closely with Dole to keep the possibility of consensus alive during the commission's deliberations in 1983. He's a very smart guy who has a firm grasp of broad principles and knows what he's trying to do. His ideas are his own. He's funny, lively, and considerate.

Wilber Mills was in a category by himself. Mills wasn't just an autocrat who exercised power, he had raw ability to back up that power. I think people recognized that he had such great ability and talents, and thus he got his way on those grounds, not merely on the grounds that he was in the seat of authority.

Those were the days before the rise of the subcommittee, an institution that has now greatly watered down the power and influence of the committee chairmen. The full committee worked on all legislation back then.

In March 1976, Mills, a Democrat from Arkansas, announced that he would not seek re-election after his term of office expired at the end of the year. Thus came to a close a 38-year distinguished career that is without parallel in our nation's history.

Sometimes history tends to remember only the most recent events on a person's record, and not the overall picture of his or her accomplishments. It is strange — and indeed dismaying — that many people now associate Mills only with his illness, alcoholism, in the early 1970's, and not with his many great achievements in the preceding three decades. It is equally dismaying that many wrongly consider Mills in the same category as other former members of Congress who were involved in moral and ethical wrongdoing, but who had never made any significant contributions to the nation.

Mills made contributions to the development of a sound and durable Social Security system and also played a significant role in other legislative areas, such as taxes and foreign trade.

Mills was Chairman of Ways and Means from 1957 to 1974, when he was forced to resign from that post. The committee was responsible for developing and considering all tax legislation, including all aspects of Social Security because it is financed through a payroll tax. It is hard now to fathom the power which Mills held. In addition to controlling the movement of tax legislation through Congress, his committee also controlled the movement of congressmen through other committees. It handed out the assignments.

When all of the powers are concentrated in an individual who is intelligent, informed, and hard-working, the combination is nearly invincible. And so it was with Mills. It is no surprise that he was so often referred to during the 1960's as the most important person in Washington in the domestic affairs area, perhaps even more influential that the President himself.

In the 1970's the power of the Ways and Means Committee was greatly reduced, as also was that of other House committee chairmen. In part, at least, this came about because of general political trends, but in the case of Mills, it was no doubt augmented by his decreased abilities due to his illness.

For many years, even before Mills' tenure as chairman, the Ways and Means Committee had dealt with legislation solely on a "full committee" basis, rather than through subcommittees. Specifically, the full committee considered all legislation in its entirety — and did so with great care, diligence, and detail, not only under Mills, but also under his predecessors. The criticisms of this procedure were that the committee's legislative output was too small and too slow, and that it permitted too much control to be exerted by the chairman because he determined what the committee should consider and when.

The so-called reforms of congressional procedures in the early 1970's changed all this, and the subcommittee procedure, which some other committees had used for a long time, was instituted for the Ways and Means Committee, beginning in 1975. Under this procedure, the responsibility for developing legislation is assigned to subcommittees, each of which has certain areas of concentration, such as Social Security, Medicare, Unemployment Insurance, and general taxation, among others. After the subcommittee makes decisions, the full committee gives a brief review of the proposed legislation before it goes to the floor of the House.

In theory the subcommittee method, by dividing up the work, was supposed to result in more legislative action. Furthermore, it was supposed to result in more democratic processes by spreading the responsibilities and the authority, instead of having them centralized in the chairman.

In most instances in the past, Social Security legislation has been developed by having the Executive Branch first send up legislative proposals. One of Mills' strong points was his insistence on having the staff, both that of the committee and that from the Executive Branch, express their views, both on policy grounds and on administrative feasibility, so that he and the committee members could more clearly see the problems and the alternative solutions. Often, he would express his views on general principles and then have the technicians develop reasonable, practical ways of accomplishing them. In the same way, too, he would accept suggestions for changes from other committee members and see that they were properly carried out. Mills did not merely talk and advocate general principles. After the technicians had developed the details, he studied the results thoroughly so that he completely understood how they would work.

Mills has been accused — mostly after his fall from power — of being dictatorial and secretive about the manner in which legislation was developed by his committee. His procedures may have had this appearance, but in my opinion such was not really the case. Mills always made extensive study of all aspects of proposals and thought of various alternative approaches. He really worked long and hard. This may well have contributed to several physical disabilities, including an intestinal ulcer, shingles, and back problems, which preceded and likely caused his drinking problem.

All of this might make it appear that Mills was merely a highly efficient, impersonal machine in developing and enacting legislation. Such was not at all the case. Unlike many legislators (most of whom weren't nearly as busy as he), Mills was readily accessible to people with an interest in the matters with which he was dealing. He always courteously, even warmly, heard their views and took them into consideration. At times he could give people the impression that he was agreeing with them, when in fact he was just nodding to show that he understood what they were saying. This left some people with the belief that he had been less than honest with them.

Mills did his homework and was blessed with a fantastic memory and a keen intelligence. At the same time, though, he relied heavily on the committee's staff and that of the Social Security Administration. It was not unusual for him to order up a report on some technical aspect of the bill under consideration, and he would take the material home at night. He would return the next day, having absorbed and understood the material in all its technical complexities.

It seems only natural, then, that Mills would treat his staff with courtesy and warmth. Still, among people of power, that behavior is unusual. He worked people hard, but he asked nothing more of them than he expected from himself.

Mills also had a legendary ability to steer legislation on the House floor to final passage. Again, he did his homework and always went into the House chamber fully prepared. His memory and quick mind served him well in debates on the floor.

He was then equally tactful and skillful in guiding the legislation through conference committees to find a compromise between differing versions of the bill passed by the House and Senate. He didn't let pride get in his way. If the Senate had come up with a better idea, he did not hesitate to accept it.

Although Mills wielded great power, he was not an authoritarian. Rather, he used his experience and his knowledge in the fine art of persuasion and influence that makes Congress tick.

His lasting legacy, and perhaps greatest achievement, was in safeguarding the financial soundness of the Social Security program. He took the long-range view of Social Security to ensure its stability for decades, and he insisted that any changes in the program should leave it in actuarial balance for 75 years. He stood firm on this. Even if he liked some proposed change, it couldn't get through his committee unless it was financed.

As a result, all of the legislation from the 1950's through the early 1970's was estimated to be soundly financed on a long-range basis. Mills also was instrumental in the passage of amendments that rounded out the benefit structure for the disabled, the retirees, and their survivors. And despite his initial opposition, Mills helped develop Medicare, deciding at long last in the mid-1960's that it was "an idea whose time had come." When it was passed, he made certain that it was financially sound, according to the best actuarial estimates available.

For these and other reasons, Mills deserves a high place among those who created and developed our Social Security program. No member of the House played a role comparable to his, and he did it for more than 20 years. The millions of current Social Security beneficiaries owe Mills a debt of gratitude, as do the many more millions who will draw benefits in the future.

CHAPTER SEVEN

A MATTER OF PRINCIPLE

Social Security in the United States is the child of Franklin D. Roosevelt, who also is considered the father of the Democratic Party as we know it today, an organization that basically stands for social welfare and liberal ideals. So it is natural that, as Social Security was formed in the 1930's and 1940's, this vast, new bureaucracy would be colonized largely by like-minded people, including men like Wilbur Cohen and Robert M. Ball.

The program admittedly did not do everything Roosevelt and his supporters wanted when the Social Security Act was passed in 1935. Whole classes of workers were not covered by Social Security, and the law contained no broad provision for health care (which we now know as Medicare).

FDR asked for as much as he could reasonably expect to get through Congress and to pass constitutional muster before a crotchety Supreme Court that was openly hostile to the New Deal.

He figured that he would come back and tidy up later. The important thing was to get the program started. Thus, from the very beginning it was a largely unwritten, but deeply ingrained part of the plan that the program would be expanded, that it would evolve as time and circumstance and money would allow.

I recognized this in 1937 when I wrote the first actuarial study of the system and considered the possibility that the program would be changed. "This probability is virtually a certainty," I wrote. "There are rarely very long periods of operation without change in a social security system. Changes will probably successively increase and decrease costs, or at least decrease the rate of increase in cost."

And as we have seen, that is exactly what has happened. Everything was fine through the Roosevelt Administration and the Truman Administration, when the Democrats in power and the Democrats in the bureaucracy were in step with each other.

It was in this environment that I went to work, a Republican among the Democrats, and I didn't particularly mind it. The reason was that my work was rather technical. It was numbers, formulas, and ledger sheets. I could get absorbed in it and derive my satisfaction from doing the best technical job I knew how, without getting too wrapped up in considering whether one policy or another was good for the nation. Maybe it can best be compared to the mindset of a surgeon, who will focus all his attention and energy on performing a successful operation without considering whether the person on the table is leading a good life or a bad one.

This grew into my somewhat peculiar notion of a bureaucrat. It's a term that's been much maligned over the years. George Wallace ran for office railing against the pointy-headed bureaucrats whom he would tame if he won. Bureaucrats are the people who are supposed to make the government work. They should put aside their personal feelings, obey the law, and follow the directions of the President of the United States, regardless of who that is.

Ours is a political system, and if someone wants to engage in politics, he or she should do it openly and honestly. To do otherwise is to cross the line that separates civil servant from saboteur.

I've never had the opinion that government was bad. I think government has its place, and there are some government activities that you've got to have. Social Security is one of them. Republicans have always been tarred with the brush of being enemies of Social Security. The system has had its enemies, and they have tended to be Republicans, but that doesn't mean all Republicans — or even most of them — want to destroy Social Security, to hack it out by its roots. It has its place and its purpose. Democrats and Republicans agree on that broad principle but disagree on its application, just as I have differed with the expansionists over the years.

Frankly, I can't say that I spent a lot of time thinking about this. I was an actuary, not a philosopher. I went to work every day, I went home every night, and I paid my bills. It never really occurred to me that the government could get out of whack with itself until the Eisenhower Administration took office. More accurately, perhaps, I didn't notice this until President Eisenhower was nearly ready to leave office.

Eisenhower himself bore no ill will toward Social Security or the legacy of FDR, his old boss (although there were some in the Administration and the party who did feel that way). But Eisenhower was not interested in expanding the program beyond providing a basic floor of protection for retirees and survivors. The Administration even opposed providing Social Security benefits to workers who are permanently disabled. The opposition from the White House was relatively mild, and the disability benefits were included in amendments that passed in 1956.

But that didn't please the expansionists in Social Security's bureaucracy to the extent that they had no further desires or goals for expansion. They believed that the program should do the whole job of providing economic security for practically everybody in the country. They engaged in an underhanded and undercover campaign to thwart the Administration's goals. They funnelled information to liberals in Congress and sometimes even wrote speeches for them. Of course, this was done in a way that didn't leave individuals' fingerprints.

It wasn't anything you could prove in a court of law, but there was no question that it was happening. Information was winding up in the hands of the Administration's political adversaries with almost lightning speed.

Once I figured out what was going on, I was offended. This was just wrong, and it was dirty. But by the time I caught on, it was really too late to do anything about it. Eisenhower was on his way out, and John F. Kennedy was on his way in. I made a note to myself, though, that if I was around to see another Republican in the White House and something like that happened again, I was going to blow the whistle.

I had a long time to wait. Kennedy and Lyndon Johnson were believers in expanding the system, so people of that philosophy prospered.

Probably the foremost expansionist within the Social Security Administration during the entire Eisenhower Administration was Robert M. Ball. In 1938 he got a job with a Social Security district office, and he quickly moved up the ladder to the central office in Baltimore. He left Social Security for a short period, but then became the staff director of the 1947 advisory council, where he did a very competent job. This council recommended a large expansion of the system that passed in 1950 and extended coverage to workers who originally had been left out, such as domestic and agricultural workers. After the council completed its work he returned to the Social Security Administration.

At the time I was Chief Actuary, so Ball and I had a great deal of contact because my office worked up the cost estimates for these changes. We got along fine.

He continued his rise through the agency, and when Kennedy took office he appointed Ball to be Commissioner of Social Security.

My friend, Wilbur Cohen, also returned to the government. Unlike Ball, who remained at Social Security throughout the Eisenhower years, Cohen had left. He played his politics out in the open. He was an unapologetic liberal Democrat, and he wouldn't have been comfortable working for the Republicans. So Wilbur did the honorable thing: he left government and went to work at the University of Michigan. Wilbur would later become Secretary of Health, Education, and Welfare under President Johnson.

The Kennedy and Johnson years were high times for the expansionists. The Social Security program had not experienced such growth since FDR was alive. These were the years that brought in Medicare, that lowered the minimum retirement age to 62 for men (as it had been lowered for women in 1956), and that relaxed requirements for disability benefits, to pay for long-term and not just permanent disability.

But nothing lasts forever, and in 1968 Richard Nixon was elected president. Wilbur returned to Ann Arbor as dean of the School of Education. I expected there would be a change in the office of commissioner, since Ball was a Democrat and the job was a political appointment.

I had even supposed that the job might come my way. After all, there were few people who knew the program better than I did. There were fewer still who had worked there longer than I had, and even fewer who were Republican. Over the last 20 years, I had worked closely with Congress and had many friends in both parties on Capitol Hill.

Unknown to me, there was at least one attempt to put my name before the President for the job. Ed Baumer, head of a Los Angeles financial marketing consulting firm, wrote to presidential assistant H.R. Haldeman on July 1, 1969, to advance my candidacy. From the context, there appears to have been prior conversations on this subject. Baumer wrote as follows:

"Dear Bob:

"Just a note to thank you ... for your very prompt reply to my inquiry by telephone from Honolulu recently.

"Your suggestion to direct a message in writing to Peter Flanigan at the White House was most appreciated. As you will recall, this concerns the belief of many business interests that Bob Myers of the Social Security system should be named as Commissioner of Social Security.

"Quite obviously, Mr. Finch is also being approached, but I believe in the value of a coordinated plan. This will enable the entire Nixon administration to understand the reasons why a very large segment of American business [and] industry is in favor of Mr. Myers."

(By way of explanation, Finch is Robert Finch, the HEW secretary, and Peter Flanigan handled personnel matters for the White House.)

I knew nothing about this effort until this letter turned up in the White House files during the course of research for this book. The campaign obviously didn't go anywhere.

But before I could move into the commissioner's office, the fellow occupying it had to go. I waited for what I believed was the inevitable resignation. It didn't happen. The Administration decided to keep Ball, a decision that, to this day, I find baffling even though I have since been told the reasons why.

It wasn't as though the Republicans were too polite to ask about one's politics. I'd been questioned about mine when Eisenhower took office. I was viewed with suspicion because the new crowd considered me a holdover from the Truman Administration. One of the new political appointees, Roswell Perkins, asked me about my politics and my motivation, and I just gave him my five-minute lecture about the integrity of the actuarial cost estimates. He didn't give me any more trouble after that, and we became pretty good friends. But he was like a lot of the political appointees who would come into office and be somewhat suspicious about the sentiments and objectivity of some of the civil servants.

The Chief Actuary's job was high enough in the Social Security Administration that it could have been filled with a political appointee. But from the very beginning of the program, virtually all of the top leadership realized that it was crucial to have independent actuarial services. They didn't just do this because it was morally right but because it made practical sense.

But it also made sense for the top job to be political, so I was stunned when Ball stayed.

Never let it be said that Bob Ball isn't quite intelligent and savvy in the ways of the world. He is a good politician in the sense of giving the appearance of being non-political. He painted himself as a long-term civil servant who would subordinate his views to those of the President. He had also wired himself tightly to the social welfare types, to organized labor, and to the academic community. These were groups that had not been supporters of Nixon in particular nor of Republicans in general. But already the Administration was looking toward the 1972 election, and the decision was made not to anger these groups by getting rid of Ball. He would stay through the first term.

It didn't take long for the trouble to start. I began to notice it right after the election in 1968, and after the Republicans came into the White House in 1969, it became more acute.

By this time, Ball and I had known each other for more than 20 years, and our relationship up to then had always been reasonably friendly. I can't say that we were pals. We weren't. But we weren't enemies either. At least not yet. However, not only did I not like his politics, I did not like the way he went about it.

It was a repeat of the games that had been played during the Eisenhower years. The policy development people had their own ideas of how things ought to be done at Social Security, and if the Visigoth in the White House didn't have the good manners to agree with them, well, they'd try to bring him along. They'd nudge him here and there, trying to get the Administration to take certain positions. If that didn't work, they'd subvert him.

As I mentioned earlier, I had decided some years before to keep an eye out for this kind of thing. It really wasn't hard to see. They abhorred Nixon and were blatant about it. Early in the Administration, the debate was over the issue of cost-of-living adjustments in Social Security benefits. Up to that time, the benefits could be raised only by an act of Congress because there was no automatic mechanism to take into account the effects that inflation would have both on the buying power of the benefits and on the amount of money collected from the payroll tax.

In an actuarial sense it's perfectly reasonable to provide a cost-of-living adjustment in the benefits. But it has to be done right to keep the system in balance. If the benefits do not go up at the same rate as inflation, then the money collected from the taxes on rising wages will pour into the trust fund and build up a surplus. If, on the other hand, the benefits rise too rapidly, then you have designed a system that will go broke.

The latter is what the expansionists under Ball wanted to do. Does this mean that they were trying to destroy Social Security? No, of course not. They knew what all of us know: Social Security will always be saved, so if they had the system living beyond its means, the government would do something to prevent a collapse. Politicians don't like to cut benefits, so they would be inclined to bring in more money by raising taxes, or dipping into the government's general fund, or a combination of those two actions. In the end you have a program that does more than it was doing before. That's expansionism.

Politically, that puts the President on the spot and forces his hand. No sane individual occupying the Oval Office is going to veto a bill for raising Social Security benefits too much. He may as well get out the cardboard boxes and start packing the cute mementos on his desk. He's not going to be there long. Nixon, regardless of whatever else you may want to say about him, was astute enough to realize this.

There was one such increase that took effect just before the 1972 election. The President had been deeply opposed to it because he thought it was too big. Nevertheless, when the bill came to his desk, he signed it. When the first checks went out with the increase in them, he had a ''stuffer'' inserted in the envelopes in which he took credit for the raise they were getting.

Ball didn't refuse to put the stuffers in, but I'm sure that at the same time he tipped the Democrats so they could raise a fuss about it. And they did. But Ball didn't do what I think he should have done under the circumstances. If he opposed the action (and he did), he should have told the White House that if they insisted on putting these misleading stuffers in the Social Security envelopes, they'd have to get another commissioner. The threat might have been enough to back them down. It also would have been up front and honest. I think those stuffers were an outrage, and strong action was called for.

But that's not the way the expansionist bureaucrats chose to operate. Their methods hadn't changed appreciably over the years. They would channel inside information to liberals in Congress to help them shape their attacks on the Administration.

I watched this charade for months after 1968 with growing anger. I went to HEW Under Secretary John G. Veneman and told him what is going on. I didn't mince words: Ball ought to be fired because he is undermining the Administration. Veneman listened and then told me something that left me completely astonished.

The Administration knew what was going on, he said. They just chose to do nothing about it. Getting rid of Ball was potentially more trouble than keeping him. They were going to tough it out until after the 1972 election, and then they'd ditch him.

I had tried to take my complaints directly to Secretary Finch but had been passed one rung down the ladder to Veneman. It was clear that avenue was a dead end, so I tried to go over the department's head and take my case straight to the White House. Clark Mollenhoff, a former prize-winning journalist and now a special counsel to the President, was assigned to hear me out. He was sympathetic, and in fact I got more support from him than I did from the political people in HEW. He encouraged me to keep on doing what I was doing, and when I left he sent me a note saying that I was doing the right thing and wishing me luck.

Although Mollenhoff told me he was very much concerned about the same things I was concerned about, he never made me any promises. I don't know if any of this was ever brought to the attention of the President. I never had any dealings with Nixon, aside from shaking hands with him once. I was never really a fan of his, but I happened to agree with his approach to Social Security.

Ball and others would say that I did what I did because I wanted to be Commissioner of Social Security, and I wasn't bashful about sticking a knife in him to get it. It's true that I wanted to be Commissioner, and it's true that I tried to derail Bob Ball. But my reasons were not personal ambition. There was an issue at stake here that was larger than me and larger than Ball.

I hesitated, to some extent, to enter this battlefield, but I just felt so strongly about what I saw as breaching the integrity of the civil service that I was going to scream about it. If it hadn't been for that, I gladly would have stayed on the job as Chief Actuary for the rest of my days. (When President Bush appointed my friend Gwen King as Commissioner, I told her, ''Now you have the *second best* job in the Social Security Administration.'')

I knew I was coming dangerously close to crossing the Rubicon, and there would be no turning back. But I'd had about all of this I could stand. So in late 1969 and early 1970, this topic started working its way into my speeches. I'd always had a fairly active schedule of public speaking, often to professional groups such as the actuarial societies, congressional town meetings, business groups, and senior citizen organizations. Outside the room where I was talking, my speeches didn't often attract that much attention.

That changed. I spoke my mind, and I named a specific person, as well as identifying the groups involved (the Office of Program Evaluation and Planning and the Office of Research and Statistics). In Washington, that's almost all you have to do to get attention. It's newsworthy because it happens so seldom. The *Washington Evening Star* concluded a story on one of my speeches with the following:

''There have been a lot of rumblings among some top Nixon appointees in recent months that career government employees in their departments and agencies have been thwarting their programs. But none of them have been willing to be quoted until now when, ironically, Myers, a career official, made the charge against his colleagues.''

I didn't pull any punches, and I even attacked Finch's wimpiness in failing to take charge and clean house: ''Wilbur Cohen might just as well still be secretary as far as any change in attitude is concerned,'' I said in one of my speeches.

This and other things that I would say during this period would, unfortunately, make Wilbur mad at me.

Cohen and Ball were like-minded on the expansion issue, but I got along well with Wilbur. Part of the reason, of course, was personality. I always thought Wilbur was very open. He spoke his mind; when he believed something, he said it. If he talked to two different groups, say a conservative business group and a labor group, he'd give the same speech. Ball, to put it kindly, was conciliatory. Wilbur knew where I stood on these things, and he knew why, so we just would agree to disagree on some things and that's it. He eventually would get over it, but for a while, he was pretty steamed.

He was still angry months later when he wrote this to me:

''I appreciate and understand that you conscientiously believe what you were stating in public. Nevertheless, I must honestly tell you that I think you were ill advised to do what you did in publicly attacking your colleagues — especially Bob Ball — and that it was not only improper for you to do so as a civil service employee but also your attacks were likely to have the effect of undermining public support for the Social Security Program and those who administer it.

''In particular I believe that many of the comments and conclusions made in your public statements have been gross exaggerations. ... I simply want you to know that the overall effect of your articles and speeches was in my opinion contrary to the best interests of the Social Security Program. Naturally, I would expect that you have a completely different view of the matter. ...

"I regret very much having to be frank with you in this letter. Our long association over 35 years is not one which I treat very lightly. ...

"I hope you will take these comments in a spirit of constructive criticism as they are so made. It is a sad experience for me to know that you are attacking unfairly your former friends and colleagues. I hope you will reconsider the tenor of your charges and try in the future to give those you criticize the same consideration you would want."

I didn't do as Wilbur suggested. He'd put it much more politely, but his advice was essentially to shut up and take it. I'd pretty much made up my mind that I would have to quit my job. That broke my heart. I loved working there. It was a great job and had a lot of responsibility. Wilbur and I agreed that a civil servant shouldn't be doing what I was doing.

Despite the press I was getting, I thought I needed a wider audience. I approached Reader's Digest with a proposal to write an article about the things I'd been saying, and the editors there agreed. We went back and forth over the wording, and my article was published in the April 1970 edition. I told Mollenhoff what I was doing and even gave him an advance copy. He wrote back a three-paragraph letter that was overall sympathetic. Again, he offered nothing and told me to keep in touch.

Here is the article, reproduced in its entirety, with permission from the Reader's Digest:

What do we want from our Social Security dollar: A basic
"floor of protection?" or an infinitely expanding — and
infinitely costly — all-purpose umbrella?

Social Security at the Crossroads

By Robert J. Myers
Chief Actuary, Social Security Administration

For the last 35 years it has been my job to provide
federal policymakers, administrators and Congress with the
cost forecasts essential to keeping the nation's Social Security program on a sound financial course. The assignment
is above politics. However, in view of my experience with
Social Security, I believe it is my duty to warn that powerful pressures are now building up, both within and outside
our government, that could soon steer Social Security down
a dangerously unsound financial course.

These pressures come from a wide range of people,
from social planners to politicians, who are all too willing
to boost retirement benefits without letting the public in on
the economic consequences. They included, among others,
some of my own associates in the Social Security Administration, certain Congressmen, theoreticians from the
academic community, labor leaders, and lobbyists who
parade as independent spokesmen for organized senior
citizens. For example:

- A State University of New York sociologist,
  Joseph H. Bunzel, tells the House Ways and
  Means Committee that the present minimum

monthly payment should be quadrupled and that the taxable wage base should be rocketed from $7,800 to $100,000 a year.

- Congress has before it a maze of proposals for vast new Social Security benefits. Many Congressmen want to provide the wherewithal by tapping general federal revenues — your tax dollars. One such advocate, Rep. Benjamin S. Rosenthal (D-N.Y.), calls for "financing the Social Security system through whatever general revenues are needed to keep it actuarially solvent."

- Speaking for 22 private welfare organizations, Philip Bernstein urges a broad and costly new pattern of benefit increases to be paid for "by the total community rather than by payroll taxes."

- Former Vice President Hubert H. Humphrey has called for a 50-percent increase in Social Security payouts, a plea echoed by former Secretary of Health, Education, and Welfare Wilbur J. Cohen.

Undoubtedly, these are sincere men. But they are united in promoting the delusion that we can forever expand the Social Security balloon, yet never fear that it will explode in our faces.

Thus, our Social Security system has come to a crossroads: Do we stay on the main, moderate road we have followed up to now? Or do we take the "high road" advocated by the expansionists (a tempting road, in an election year, for some politicians of both parties)?

Before answering, it might be wise to consider what Social Security originally set out to accomplish.

Floor of Protection. Unlike private insurance, which pays off from the investment of your premiums, Social Security chiefly transfers to non-working beneficiaries a tax collected on the payrolls of the nation's workers. These workers contribute in the reasonable expectation that there will be younger workers willing to do the same for them in years to come. Moderate legislators, who have sought to safeguard development of the system, have worked to limit Social Security to what initially was called a "basic floor of protection." This meant keeping costs low enough to encourage development of private savings and investment, while at the same time assuring Social Security benefits which when combined with these other anticipated resources, would be high enough to enable most Americans to maintain at least an acceptable minimum standard of living on retiring or becoming permanently disabled.

The private investments that have resulted from this moderate approach speak for themselves. Individual Americans now own about 34 million homes, compared with 12 million 40 years ago. In that same period, their life insurance in force has climbed from $102 billion to $1,300 billion; personal savings from $3 billion to more than $40 billion a year. The number of people with private hospital insurance has increased from just 12 million in 1940 to 170 million now. Today about 29 million individuals are protected by $125 billion invested in private pension and deferred profit-sharing plans. Only about seven percent of all our 25 million Social Security beneficiaries now require an additional check from public-welfare funds in order to meet their basic needs. Surely any Social

Security setup that can accomplish this must be regarded as generally adequate.

Through the years this basic floor-of-protection concept has permitted benefit rises to keep up-to-date with economic changes. It has also permitted inequities to be ironed out and refinements to be made. This process should continue. For example, in an era of skilled-labor shortage there is certainly room for re-examination of that portion of the law that curtails or completely shuts off a man's Social Security benefits if he wants to continue working after his 65th birthday — and then requires him to continue to pay Social Security taxes. President Nixon has proposed certain improvements in this area.

Conflict of Philosophies. However, simple adjustments to keep the basic system up-to-date are not at all what the expansionists have in mind. The AFL-CIO, a prime source of expansion pressure, candidly states that between the moderates and the expansionists "the conflict is not a simple battle of numbers; it is a conflict of philosophies." In place of a basic floor of protection, the AFL-CIO argues that the Social Security system alone "should provide the basic retirement system by which the elderly can live out their lives in dignity and economic security."

In the past, Congress has held the expansionists in check, and thus kept the system actuarially sound. But by last year the expansionists were able to get the Senate to adopt, by a 48 to 41 vote, a so-called "Christmas tree" measure that nearly doubled the minimum Social Security payment — and jumped the taxable wage base from $7,800 to $12,000. Only through compromise were the House-Senate conferees on this legislation, under the leadership of House Ways and Means Committee Chairman Wilbur D. Mills and his senior Republican associate, Rep. John W.

Byrnes, able to slice away at some of the Senate innovations and send to the White House a bill which, for the time being, held the expansionists to a 15-percent across-the-board increase in current Social Security benefits.

Even so, this one piece of "emergency" legislation will necessitate $4.2 billion of additional outlays for 1970 alone. Over the years, this change will use up the actuarial surplus of the Social Security trust fund, which is all of the taxes collected through the years that are in excess of required disbursements. President Nixon had intended that this surplus not only should finance his proposal for a ten-percent hike in benefits (which would have adequately offset increased living costs to date), but also should pay for his other proposed improvements: a better deal for people over 65 who want to continue working; equitable increases in widows' pensions; a temporary reduction in the Social Security tax rate that workers must pay; rescuing Medicare from a financial dilemma.

Torch of Promise. What now? Congress must reopen the entire Social Security package and find ways to bring in more money. President Nixon has already called for raising the taxable wage base to $9,000 in 1971, 12 months earlier than he had previously recommended. But even this will not be enough to sufficiently bolster Medicare's seriously underfinanced hospital insurance, which at present levels of financing will go broke by late 1972.

Crisis or no crisis, however, the expansionists are back again at the Capitol, pulling and shoving to promote enormously expensive new schemes. No fewer than 892 bills to change Social Security were dropped into the House legislative hopper during the first session of this Congress. Many of these proposals would so balloon benefits that taxes would also have to soar. But one bill stands out as the expansionists' torch of promise. It was introduced by Rep. Jacob H. Gilbert of New York, and is backed by the National Council of Senior Citizens, which has kept up an incessant clamor for ever larger Social Security payments as essential to combat what it considers to be "destitution." In fact, this nationwide lobbying organization has boasted that Representative Gilbert "consulted with officers of the National Council in designing every feature of the bill."

If the Gilbert bill were to pass (which is highly unlikely), it would all by itself raise last year's Social Security benefits by about 50 percent. The minimum of $120 a month would go to many individuals who weren't part of the regular labor force but, as in the case of some wives and retired government employees (who are not covered by Social Security), have accepted temporary part-time jobs just to qualify for a minimum benefit. A retired couple who under last year's law could collect a maximum of $376 a month would take in as much as $805 instead; for a widow with one child the increase would be from $307 to $805. Doctors' calls and drugs from the neighborhood pharmacy would be largely free to all retirees; there would be no restraining premiums to pay.

All this is just the beginning. The ultimate aim of the expansionists, as disclosed by Walter P. Reuther, co-chairman of the powerful Alliance for Labor Action, includes a Social Security annuity of as much as $10,000 a year, amounting to a full two-thirds of a beneficiary's highest ten years of "covered" pre-retirement earnings.

What is astounding is that so little is said about the cost of this sort of expansion. The fact is that every additional benefit that is handed out to 25 million retirees must be paid for by taxing the 73 million persons who do work, along with their employers. By the end of the current decade, for example, the cost to the taxpayers of providing the benefits called for by the Gilbert bill would mount to about $135 billion a year. The taxable base would increase to $15,000 in 1972 and probably to about $20,400 by 1980. Direct Social Security taxes would be increased from a top of $920 a year now scheduled for 1987 to as much as $2,448 by 1980, shared equally between employee and employer. (Self-employed persons would pay $1,632 by 1980.) Even these colossal taxes would fall one-third — or $45 billion — short of paying the annual bill. Where, pray, would this additional cash come from?

The Greatest Dangers. Commissioner of Social Security Robert M. Ball has raised the question of ''whether some of the additional financing should come from general revenues.'' This means that after you pay as high a Social Security tax as can be directly squeezed out of you, you'll have to hand over ever bigger federal income and other taxes so as to provide a Social Security subsidy — a subsidy that will be as difficult to control as any other that finds its way into the federal bureaucracy.

And give heed to this: The march of these expansionists will not be halted simply by non-adoption of the current Gilbert bill or by failure of any other single piece of legislation. Their long-range strategy is to lay down a barrage of demands, win what they can through compromise, then, even before the ink is dry on the legislation, begin anew the advance which brings them ever closer to their goals.

What makes all this so important just now is that our Social Security system has virtually matured, so that there is a good balance between costs levied on the economy and the resulting benefits. Thus, we've arrived at a crossroads for Social Security. It would seem a good time to heed the advice of the late Supreme Court Justice Louis Brandeis:

"Experience should teach us," he said, "to be most on our guard to protect liberty when the government's purposes are beneficent. The greatest dangers to liberty lurk in insidious encroachment by men of zeal, well meaning but without understanding."

I had nailed my theses to the church door, and I didn't expect to get away with it any more than Martin Luther did. In all of this, I never discussed the subject directly with Ball. I couldn't see what the point would be. He knew what he was doing.

On April 14, 1970, I submitted my letter of resignation to Secretary Finch, which is reproduced below (and was printed in the *Congressional Record* for June 3, page S-8267).

Dear Mr. Secretary:

It is with the utmost regret that I am constrained to submit my resignation as Chief Actuary of the Social Security Administration.

I am deeply concerned about the welfare of the Nation, and I wish to serve the Nixon Administration and the Congress to the best of my ability. I believe that I can best serve these causes by remaining in my present position until the President signs the Social Security bill which will result from the pending Congressional deliberations.

Therefore, I have not set a definite date for my resignation. If you believe that my continued presence is not in the best interests of the Department, I will be glad to make my resignation effective at any earlier date. I would appreciate your informing me as to your views on this matter.

I wish to make it clear they my resignation is by no means related to my views on the pending Social Security legislation. In fact, the situation is quite the opposite. I strongly believe that the President's proposal is an excellent one, including its sound financing. It is certainly the most progressive, forward step taken in the Social Security field in many years.

I believe that the President's proposal very well conforms with, and implements, the moderate philosophy of Social Security. It is a progressive, forward step that would prevent future over-expansion of the program, which would destroy private efforts in the economic security field and thus lead to serious consequences insofar as our national economy is concerned.

I should also add that now — as at all previous times during my 35 years of actuarial service with the Social Security program — no one has made any attempt whatsoever to influence or sway the technical actuarial cost estimates for the existing program or any proposed changes therein.

The question might well be raised as to why I believe, in all conscience and integrity, that I must resign. I have previously talked with you about my strong personal beliefs and have given you much supporting factual evidence to substantiate my views — namely, that certain of the top policy-making officials of the Social Security Administration (who are holdovers from the Johnson Administration) have strong beliefs in the desirability — even the necessity

— of the public sector taking over virtually all economic security provisions for the entire population and thus eliminating private efforts in this area. It seems to me that this viewpoint is completely alien to that of the Nixon Administration.

Further, and equally important, it is my deeply-held conviction, as I have expressed to you a number of times in the past, that these officials of the Social Security Administration have not — and will not — faithfully and vigorously serve the Nixon Administration. Rather, they will exert their efforts to expand the Social Security program as much as possible by aiding and supporting any individuals and organizations that are of this expansionist conviction. Such anachronistic actions took place extensively during the Eisenhower Administration — against its political views. Such working at cross purposes with the Nixon Administration has occurred in the past year, and is still occurring, although to a somewhat limited extent so far. I have brought to your attention, on several occasions, the fact that the Social Security Administration is excessively wasteful by spending far too much time and money in performing research, conducting program planning, and collecting statistics in a manner that is not only nonproductive of sufficient worthwhile results, but also inimical to what I understand to be the philosophy and goals of the Nixon Administration.

Undoubtedly, there will be those who will say that I am taking this action solely or largely because I seek enhanced personal recognition. This is not the case. There is no position of any type that I would rather serve in than my present one, and I am not happy to have to leave it.

Evidently, no credence is placed in what I have related to you personally or in other evidence that I have furnished

you on this matter, which has such an important effect on
the future of the Social Security program. Therefore, I
must, in good conscience and personal integrity, resign. It
is especially dismaying to me to have to take this action,
because I had hoped to serve the Nixon Administration not
only with competence and integrity — as I had tried to
serve all previous Administrations — but also with great
enthusiasm, since I strongly believe in its philosophy and
goals.

Sincerely yours,

Oh, yes, I also mailed out almost 150 copies of the letter
to people inside and outside the government. Then I sat back and
waited for somebody to say something.

Nothing!

Not a word. The silence was eerie. In the absence of
other instructions, I just kept going to work as though nothing had
happened. A week later, I sent Finch a memo repeating the
complaints in my letter of resignation and adding a couple more.
One that especially irked me was the way I thought Ball was trying
to steer the Advisory Council on Social Security by providing the
members with selective information designed to lead them to a
particular and pre-chosen conclusion.

I did not approve of this thumb-on-the-scale style of
management. In all of the Social Security Administration, I was
more in a position that others to nudge policies one way or
another. A tiny change in assumptions in one place, a shaded
percentage in another, and millions of dollars can turn into
billions. I could, in other words, put my thumb on the scale and
do it in such a way that I probably wouldn't get caught. And yet

I just believed that this is something that you don't do. At the same time, nobody in the government ever tried to pressure me to cook the numbers, nor did anyone make a direct attempt to influence the figures.

Maybe it was because of high ideals, and maybe it was because I realized that if you do ever get caught — just once — you're done. Once an actuary's credibility is shot, there's nothing left, so I don't want to sound too noble here. I just realized that if you're going to do it, you've got to do it right. You've got to be consistent, and you've got to have people who believe that you are doing it right. Besides, getting caught was always a possibility. From time to time, actuaries from private industry would be brought in to audit our work and make sure that everything was on the up and up. We always got a clean bill of health.

So as I approached what I knew would be the end of my government service, having kept myself clean all these years, I was especially ticked when it appeared that my superiors — the very people responsible for the double-dealing that was driving me out of my job — were questioning my integrity.

"I have discussed in some detail other matters indicating what appears to me to be a complete lack of faith in me — other than perhaps for my actuarial cost-estimating function — by you and the Under Secretary, so it will suffice here only to mention them," I wrote in the memo to Finch. "These items include establishing a committee to review my Medicare cost estimates without any discussion with me before the action was completed.

"In summary then, I see no other course of action that is possible for me to take other than as outlined in my letter of April 14."

I waited again. Silence.

Maybe my action was completely alien to their way of thinking. Quitting over a matter of principle is not the way things are done in this government. People tend to leave either because they're in trouble or because they receive a better offer.

I realized that if you're trying to get ahead politically often you've got to do, not what you think is right, but what is the political course of action at the time. I think I've had some liability over the years because I've felt compelled to speak my mind. I've been a team player, but I won't stick with it if I have to follow a course of action that I believe is flawed. And I thought it was just plain wrong to sweep this under the rug.

Charlotte Crenson, a very good friend at the Social Security Administration who was the press officer at the time, said, "Look, you shouldn't be doing this. You're going to ruin yourself. You'll never be heard of again." That opinion was widely shared by my friends inside the agency.

In the meantime, I had some speaking engagements to keep, and a month after my memo to Finch, I sent Ball a request for travel orders. Nothing exotic, just Virginia Beach, Chicago, and Miami Beach, and I was only going to be gone a couple of days. The problem was that my engagement in Miami Beach (where I was to give a speech entitled "Social Security after 33 Years — Its Strengths, Its Weaknesses, and Its Direction") conflicted with a meeting of the Advisory Council on Social Security.

I was aware of this, but the council wasn't going to be talking about anything that really required me to be there. If they had any questions of an actuarial nature, there'd be someone present from my office who could answer them.

I didn't have to wait long for a reply. The next day, I got a memo from Ball. Across the top it said "R U S H." He was telling me that I couldn't go to give the speeches because I had to be at that meeting.

Sure. These guys had been ignoring me for more than a year, and suddenly I was supposed to believe that I was indispensable. In fact, they needed me so badly that Ball suggested I cancel my speaking engagements for the next few weeks.

"Should these organizations wish it, I am sure we can arrange for some other Social Security official to take your place on the program," Ball wrote.

I sent him back a note the same day, telling him, essentially, to take a long walk in a cold rain.

"I consider that the personal commitments that I have for this coming week are far more important for the welfare of the country than any official duties that might arise during that time," I wrote. "Moreover, this particular session of the Advisory Council is not at all a crucial one. ... Accordingly, I shall not be in the office May 25-28."

Ball sent a note back the same day:

"As long as you are an employee of the Social Security Administration, I must insist on your performing your duties as chief actuary. These duties include the very important work now going on with the Advisory Council on Social Security. I am, therefore, not approving either the annual leave or the leave without pay which you requested, and I expect you to attend the Council meeting and be available to help prepare for the meeting."

Amazing! Somebody in Social Security had finally grown a spine. I couldn't believe that they had let me get away with this for so long. If I were Bob Ball, I would have slapped me down. Hard! But until this last salvo of paper, he never said a word, and even then he didn't address the central issue. I was, in a word, insubordinate. I can only guess at his motivation, but it appears to me that Ball didn't want to get into a messy public display of firing me, any more than Nixon wanted to get into a messy public display of firing him.

Anyway, I stuck to my guns. I was leaving town. End of discussion. Well, at that, Ball went to his boss and complained. Finch had since left the department and went to work at the White

House as a counselor to the President, so Ball was taking his case up with the acting secretary, Veneman.

On May 25, I got a three-sentence letter from Veneman:

"In reply to your letter of April 14, 1970, I am accepting your resignation effective as of today. Your application for retirement benefits is being forwarded to you by the Social Security Administration.

"Commissioner Ball joins me in commending you for your many contributions to the Social Security program during your some 34 years of government service and in wishing you a long and enjoyable retirement."

I wasn't quite done yet. I knew that the next move for them would be to crank up the agency's publicity mill. That would take them a while. My press release got to the news media a day before theirs did and emphasized that this was not a matter of "retirement".

It was really pretty simple. I sent out copies of my letter of resignation along with a cover sheet that said Ball "attempted, in vain, to muffle and intimidate me with regard to three speeches that I was making in support of the Nixon Administration's position on Social Security legislation."

Then I left town to make my speeches.

The news was getting the bounce I had hoped for. "Social Security Aide Charges Sabotage," was the headline in *The Milwaukee Journal*. My letter of resignation was picked up and reprinted a number of times in the *Congressional Record*.

I didn't have any sleepless nights over what I'd done, but it was still unsettling, for both Rudy and me. There was no doubt in my mind that I'd be able to earn a living. I knew there would be offers coming in, and there were. In fact there's been a steady and fairly lucrative stream of them in the more than two decades that have passed since I quit.

Still, you don't work some place that long, have it become a part of your life, and then walk away from it without some misgivings.

The mail that I started getting almost immediately was a real comfort.

My old boss, W.R. Williamson, who quit the Social Security Administration in 1947 because of his deep philosophical differences, dropped me a line to tell me there is life after leaving the government.

"You will have a freer situation on the outside, and your 'firing' might be what was needed for doing a little house-cleaning!" he wrote. "I hope you will find the 'pot of gold' at the end of the rainbow, too! I really do think 'God's in his heaven' still and that a bit of prayer helps."

Williamson's former assistant at Social Security, Dorrance Bronson, also wrote to me.

"I strongly feel that you carried out an extremely courageous operation in resigning as you did," Bronson wrote. "I am convinced that you got a lousy, shabby deal from Bob Ball (whom I never trusted) and Veneman and Finch."

Arthur Altmeyer, the first commissioner of Social Security, wrote to say he was saddened by what had happened and thought that I was out of line to question my colleagues' integrity.

"I am quite sure that you and I would not always agree as to how far we should go in changing the existing law; but I am equally sure that I could depend upon you to give me the relevant facts and arguments upon which to form a judgment," Altmeyer wrote. "In fact, I think I might find you more helpful if you disagreed because that would induce me to take a second look before I made a decision."

Wilbur Cohen thought I'd lost my marbles.

"I think your expositions have tended to be political, emotional and unactuarial," he wrote. "Your 'political' endorsement of the Nixon Administration in your writings is certainly one which you are entitled to make, but I believe it may serve to limit your usefulness as an actuary and a social security expert. This I regret.''

Fortunately, Wilbur's fears for my future did not come to pass. One other thing also never came to pass: I never got to be Commissioner of Social Security.

After the 1972 election, Ball went over the side, just like Veneman said he would. Ball, of course, says he wasn't fired; he'd just decided it was time to leave. Maybe. But I think it's more than a coincidence that his timetable fit the one the Administration had laid out for him years earlier.

Now that there was an opening for the commissioner's job, it's legitimate to ask why the Nixon Administration didn't turn to me. The answer is that I wasn't seen as being politically stable enough. Resigning as I did angered some and spooked others.

I didn't follow instructions. The Administration wanted to wait before it put an ax in Bob Ball's back. Until then, I was supposed to sit quietly. I didn't do that, and in the inverted logic of Washington, my defense of the Administration was seen as an act of disloyalty by the very people I was supporting.

These were the guys who went on to later fame in the Watergate scandal for drawing up an ''enemies list.'' Maybe this was all they were capable of.

They sure couldn't figure out who their friends were.

Epilogue

After the heartbreak of leaving the Social Security Administration, I by no means became a sulking recluse. I was honored by being appointed a full professor with tenure at Temple University, where I taught mostly — guess what — Social Security. I remained at Temple until I reached the compulsory retirement age of 67. I then continued in academia as a visiting professor at Howard University.

At the same time, I kept hold of the "Social Security bear's tail" by closely following the experience and legislative developments in the Social Security and Medicare fields. Further, I had continuing consulting connections with several groups — the Republican members of both the House Ways and Means Committee and the Senate Finance Committee, the American Council of Life Insurance, the American Medical Association, Meidinger, Inc. (now merged with William M. Mercer, Inc.), and the National Association of Life Underwriters. And there were many exciting foreign technical assistance missions (see next chapter).

CHAPTER EIGHT

A WORLD TOUR

We were having lunch with the administrator of Grenada's social security system on a balmy October day in 1983. Rudy and I had been on the island for a week while I examined its social security system and prepared a report for the Organization of American States, with Rudy acting as my secretary (as she was on most of my foreign missions over the years).

I had done this sort of thing a lot, both before and after I'd left the government. This assignment didn't seem too unusual or mathematically difficult.

Until the gunfire broke out.

Our meal was interrupted by a loud noise from the city. It was the sound of a military takeover of the government. Our host had casually mentioned to us upon our arrival nearly a week earlier that Prime Minister Maurice Bishop was under house arrest.

Bishop himself had seized power in Grenada in a coup in the spring of 1979. He was a leftist and was supported by the communist government of Cuba, but apparently he wasn't communist enough to suit some members of his military. They had now turned on him.

That seemed to be of little interest to this mild-mannered pensioner from the United States, who was on the island to ply his actuarial science on the country's retirement system. Besides, the OAS had given me explicit instructions to keep my nose out of Grenada's politics and stick to looking at its social insurance operation.

But the politics was hard to ignore. Almost throughout the time we were there, people were out demonstrating in the streets, and there were frequent power blackouts.

We were having lunch with our host to say good-bye. We'd wrapped up our work, and we were catching the 5 o'clock plane to get out of there before anything bad happened.

Now there was this gunfire, rifles and cannons. Flames and smoke appeared over the city. An attempt was being made to free Bishop and his ministers by force. It failed, and the prime minister and some members of his Cabinet were executed that night. Grenada's government, or at least the guys in charge at the moment, imposed a round-the-clock curfew.

As Americans on the island we were more than curiosities. We were now regarded with suspicion, and my having worked most of my life for the government may simply have fed the fantasy. (Some of our friends still josh us that I was there for the CIA to help prepare for a U.S. invasion.)

Needless to say, all of this put a kink in our travel plans. We, as well as all other guests at our hotel, the Spice Island Inn, were subject to the same martial law as applied throughout the island. The hotel was a nice place on a pretty stretch of beach. We were warned that if we walked out the front door and stepped into the street, we could be shot on sight, but we were free to go out to the beach. For the next four days, we spent a lot of time there, taking short walks and swimming in the ocean and in the small private pool that went along with our cottage.

We also could talk to students at a medical college next door. Most of them were Americans, and when they weren't worrying about becoming lifeless victims of the island's anarchy, they fretted over the money they thought that they had blown on trying to become doctors.

Reliable news was hard to come by. The government radio station was schizophrenic. When it wasn't babbling hysterically over its belief in an imminent U.S. invasion, it was engaged in the sort of Orwellian reporting that was a hallmark of Marxist journalism: it said everything was fine. It also reminded people that martial law was in effect, and they ought to stay home.

There was a representative there from the OAS who had diplomatic immunity, so he could come and go despite the curfew. Often he couldn't bring anything but reassurance. On the fourth day, the curfew was relaxed and the OAS representative drove us to the airport, where he hoped to get us on an outgoing plane.

The airport was a mad-house scene, just like in the movies, when crowds of people are trying to escape what they fear may be their doom. Our protector managed to get us on a six-passenger plane chartered by a bank for its local manager and his wife and two children. So at sunset our plane — the last of the very few to get out — took off for St. Lucia, where we transferred to a commercial flight to Barbados. Thus we were able to escape Grenada unharmed, although a bit shaken by our experience.

At daybreak the next day our fondest hopes and the Grenadian military's worst nightmare came true: The U.S. military landed.

This wasn't my first trip to a war zone. I had gone to South Vietnam in 1969, where I had written a report advising the government on what to do about its social security system after it won the war. My advice to Grenada seems to have gotten better use.

So what am I doing kibitzing in other countries' affairs? The fact is that social security is a global phenomenon. Almost every country in the world — even the poorest ones — have some form of it and employ it with varying degrees of success.

The United States, despite our pride in our ingenuity, did not invent the idea. Actually, the notion of social security is quite European. Whereas our system didn't exist until 1935, Germany, under the leadership of Otto von Bismarck, began developing social insurance in the 1880's. The idea spread across Europe by the early part of this century.

In the Americas, Chile led the way, putting a program into effect in 1924. Brazil, Ecuador, Peru, and Uruguay also started social security systems before or about the same time as the United States.

What we have in this country, however, is a system that works and has from the day it began. It has never missed a month without sending out checks on time or otherwise failed to do its job. So even though we didn't invent social security, we have an expertise in it that is relatively unmatched, and we have a contribution to make by advising other nations on ways to improve their systems.

This does not mean that we try to transplant the U.S. system in other countries. What works well for us may be a disaster for them. They may not, for example, have the personnel, or training or computer horsepower that it takes to track the entire employment history of every one of their citizens.

These programs also are a reflection of the society in which they exist. The economy, the nature of the family, the role of women, history, and even religion can have an effect on how the program is structured.

I started getting international assignments in the late 1940's, traveling abroad to attend meetings or to give technical assistance to a government that had asked for help. Initially I went under the auspices of the U.S. government, but later on until the 1980's I went at the behest of the Organization of American States.

Although the OAS seems to have gotten out of the business of assisting nations on their social security systems, it had been one of two international organizations for years that did this. The other is the International Labor Office, originally founded as part of the League of Nations and now affiliated with the United Nations. Recently the World Bank and the Inter-American Development Bank have entered this field.

Although it is an unfailingly well-intended organization, the ILO often seeks to foster social insurance by transplanting European methods. For reasons already mentioned here, this isn't always a good idea, so in that respect the ILO and I philosophically part company.

Anyhow, I've been at this for a while, and like anything else, you get better at these things with practice. I'd learned what to look for and what questions to ask. It's also important to get a real feel for how the system works — or doesn't. You can't get that from reading a description or having somebody tell you about the law. I'd ask to be shown the department where records were posted. I wanted to see what kind of records they kept, and how they were kept. I'd want to see what a claims form looked like and be told how it was processed. I also wanted to scrutinize a few completed cases.

I do this in a few weeks, usually less than a month. I've been approached over the years by a number of organizations, such as the World Bank, asking me to go to this or that country for six months and make a study of their social security system. As much as I like to travel, I decline. I don't have the time to spend six months anywhere. Besides, I can usually get done in three weeks what they think ought to take me half a year.

Obviously in a week or two I can't do any in-depth work. To make a real actuarial study and analysis would take a year. I get what you might call actuarial impressions. Sometimes these countries would have reports from the ILO, which had sent somebody there for a long time. I would look at their report and see what I thought of the assumptions which they made. I would assume that they could do the arithmetic correctly. But I have a feel for what costs are. When I see the provisions of a plan — the retirement age, the benefit level, and the contribution conditions — I have a feeling as to whether the program is adequately financed. I have an informed guess, you might say, but it's really pretty informed.

Another problem you have to look at in these countries is what their investments are in. Are they good investments or have they deteriorated with inflation? In many of these plans — unlike the United States — the government contributes to the retirement fund from its general revenues. But sometimes the government doesn't pay, and although it's on the books, do you count the government promise as an asset?

Officials in these countries sometimes want an outside person to criticize the government. Maybe the government people don't want to criticize the minister of the treasury, but if somebody else does it from the outside, it might carry more weight.

I'd have to point out that the government isn't living up to its obligation, without necessarily criticizing the system. If the government wants to pay for part of the program and carries through on the promise, fine. But if it doesn't, then the financial underpinnings of the system are simply fiction. In that case the government should withdraw its promised financing from the plan and charge the employers and employees more because some day that money will have to be paid out. An empty promise won't get the checks written.

The nations of Eastern Europe, now emerging from the empty promise of communism, are taking stock of their social insurance programs. And they're getting lots of advice.

The private Western foundations, like the Ford Foundation, are just throwing money at Eastern Europe to have all these conferences now. I think an awful lot of money is being wasted.

I attended a meeting in Vienna paid for by the Ford Foundation, where representatives of Czechoslovakia, Hungary and Poland attended. They've had systems for years, much longer than we have. Some of them are pretty good in some ways. Some people who are not directly associated with the program have the idea that they ought to completely turn the system upside down and start over again. I'm not so sure that's a good idea.

The systems have their problems, though. They're costly because they have low retirement ages and no retirement test. Under this situation, a worker reaches age 55 and starts drawing a pension, although still going to work every day as for the past 35 years.

The disability provisions are often out of whack because many able-bodied people are drawing disability benefits. It acts more like unemployment insurance. Even there, they let people go on working.

In relative terms, as a percentage of wages, the level of benefits is high. That's because wages are so low. When people retire they still need shelter and food. There's a minimum level below which you can't go, or the retirement benefits just won't be meaningful.

In the past, these programs were often partly financed by payroll taxes on the employer and partly from general revenues from the government to make up the deficits. These programs currently are thinking of having employee contributions, in part, to make people aware of the cost of the system.

The communist states didn't plan very well. That's the problem with a so-called planned economy. They don't even call it that anymore. They used to talk about the market economy in the capitalist countries as against their planned economy. Now they call it the command economy. I think the reason is that "planned" is a good word, but "command" is closer to the truth.

As these nations are now turning to the West for advice, not all of what they're getting is high quality. They had a lot of people brought over from the United States at this meeting in Vienna. There was some guy from Harvard who's supposed to be an expert on pensions. He was *surprised* to learn that the United States is increasing the retirement age under Social Security, and it is already in the law!

Over the years I've traveled to some three dozen countries to examine their systems. The remainder of this chapter describes some of what I have learned along the way.

Greece

I went there in 1948 as my first overseas mission. Greece was a shambles after the war, and its social security system, which must have been an administrative monstrosity on its best day, was in utter disrepair.

In its ancient history, Greece was a collection of city-states isolated by rugged terrain. These city-states sometimes got together, but only to go to war with each other. In modern times, this is how their social security program worked. The Greek system actually was some 30 different systems. There was, for example, a system for bank workers in Athens and another system for bank workers in Salonika. Of course, the more powerful economic groups had the best systems. The general workers had poor systems.

Greece asked the United States for help, and the battle plan was for us to arrive in two waves. I was to be the first ashore to make a study of the system, figure out how it operated, gather statistics, and write a report for the next wave, the administrative people who were going to help fix things.

The Greek system eventually was reformed, but not completely. Our administrative people went over there, and I think they were a big help in giving the Greeks suggestions for better administrative procedures and how to do more things by machine and less by hand. It's awfully hard to put a system back together when it's broken up into a lot of parts.

Japan

I went here for five weeks in late 1950 as an outgrowth of the U.S. postwar occupation. After the war, the United States and its victorious general, Douglas MacArthur, combed through Japanese society and particularly its form of government to root out the undemocratic principles that had allowed a mysterious emperor and zealous militarists to lay waste to a considerable portion of the planet.

My tiny corner of this was to look at the civil service retirement system. I was given a desk in the building that was formerly the headquarters of the Dai Ichi Mutual Life Insurance Company. It was just across the street from the grounds of the Imperial Palace in downtown Tokyo, and now it was MacArthur's headquarters. My desk was in a big room on the same floor as the general's office, and it was not unusual for me to look up and see him and his entourage coming or going.

There was a lot of this coming and going when I first got there. Brass was everywhere, with people in a hurry and obviously agitated. On top of overhauling Japan, MacArthur was also running the war in Korea. That winter was when the war started to go badly, and all the running around I saw was when the Red Chinese arrived in force and crossed the border in the dark. They then began pushing the United Nations troops into the sea.

Understandably, my project was barely a blip on MacArthur's radar screen. The occupation authorities were interested in the retirement system of the Japanese civil service because it seemed to allow a wide opening into the government for corruption and undue corporate influence.

The retirement ages for the very highest civil servants were between 45 and 50. This was low even by Japanese standards. The usual retirement age there was between 55 and 60. This was because mortality was then high, although it has since become the lowest in the world.

This early retirement, which applied only to a thin layer of officials at the very top of Japan's government, gave an open door to corporations, which would come in a couple of years before their retirement and offer to hire them at big salaries when they did retire. So for the last few years of their government service, and usually at the height of their power, these officials would be doing things in the interest of the corporations. This is how the big monopolies sort of controlled the government.

They had a reasonably good retirement system; the benefits were in line. It was just that the retirement ages were on the low side.

The Japanese, as best I could tell, were quite open about what the plan was. I had to work through interpreters because I couldn't speak or read Japanese, and these people did a conscientious, honest job. If anyone asked what I was after, I would tell them that I was just studying their retirement system. I'd let it go at that.

I had to do a little bit of digging, and when I investigated, I found out this situation was quite possible. I didn't find the hard evidence that this was happening, although that's what I was told. I just found that the system permitted it to occur.

Going to Japan so soon after the war was a strange experience. For years they had been the enemy. Now, for five weeks, I was quartered at Tokyo's famous Imperial Hotel. It was a very interesting old hotel that was designed by Frank Lloyd Wright and built just after World War I. Wright used architectural techniques considered unsafe, but because of them the hotel had survived a big earthquake that hit Tokyo in 1923. It was taken over by the U.S. military, and I stayed there, I think, for $5 a day and meals at $1 apiece. It sounds like a pittance, but my government per diem was just $8 at the time, so there wasn't much left over.

Even though the war was still a fresh memory, I never felt any animosity on the part of the Japanese people. They were open and friendly.

One day I got a peculiar invitation from the "grand master of the ceremonies" of the Imperial Household, asking me to attend a "duck netting party" at 9:30 on a Sunday morning.

I took a military car to the Imperial Grounds, where my fellow duck netters and I gathered at a pavilion near a summer house on that cool morning in late November.

This was an honor, I was told.

This was weird, I thought.

Duck netting was not a popular sport, and it's easy to see why the Japanese have since taken up baseball and golf.

The object of the sport, as its name implies, is to net a duck. It's sort of the Japanese equivalent of fox hunting, a pointless weekend diversion for the idle rich at the expense of some smaller-brained creature.

We were given big nets on long poles. Then we marched into an open field and stood in two lines behind a tall screen at the end of a canal. On a signal from the master of the hunt, we were instructed to take positions along the canal "quickly but quietly" so as not to scare the ducks.

The canal was on the other side of an embankment, so you couldn't really see it, and the ducks couldn't see that there were a bunch of people with nets waiting for them. At some point, they started to fly. I think somebody was throwing them up in the air.

As the ducks would fly off, we would swat at them with these giant nets. I caught a duck. It wasn't hard. In my youth I'd played lacrosse.

After a period of frantic quacking and flapping and swatting, it was over. Then we stood around and had drinks while we talked over our experience and the finer points of the game. Then lunch was served. Duck.

Another sidelight to this trip was a meeting with some Japanese actuaries. Japan has always been one of the countries that had actuaries because they had good mathematicians. They sort of copied the British and American structure of having a society of actuaries and examinations.

These fellows worked for insurance companies. I was surprised to learn from them how quickly the Japanese people had their confidence in the private life insurance system restored after the war. It was almost as though their faith had never been shaken.

It had good reason to be. Inflation chewed up the value of the policies and reduced the yen to almost nothing. The only thing for the government to do was start over with another currency, a new yen. After years of paying premiums and banking on these policies, the Japanese had lost everything, but when the new yens were issued, people went out and bought new policies. It was a remarkable expression of faith and another of many indications of the way they save so well.

Reform of the Japanese insurance industry, by the way, was another outgrowth of the U.S. occupation. At our insistence, all of the companies were converted into mutual companies, which operate sort of like cooperatives and are owned by their policyholders. Until then, many of the large Japanese companies were stock companies, owned by their shareholders. (Most large U.S. companies are mutuals.)

I learned something else about Japan while I was there. We had done a great deal for them in the field of public health and sanitation. It is a theory of mine that this is a major reason why their mortality improved so much after the war. Japan used to be a relatively high mortality country. Now it has the lowest mortality in the world, even a little lower than the Scandinavian countries.

The Japanese always tried to be very sanitary. When they go into a house, for example, they take off their shoes. But even so, they didn't have good public health conditions. This is one thing we did for Japan, and I'm not sure that anybody has given us much credit for it.

How much of a role this played I can't prove, but it was certainly an important element. To do a study like that would be a full-time matter for a year or two. It can make an interesting general study, but you can't always prove exactly why things happen.

Before I left Japan, I was ushered into MacArthur's office to give him an oral report on my findings. Somebody went with me to handle the introductions. Although I'd seen him around the office, we'd never spoken, and it was kind of a thrill to meet this great hero of the war.

He was sitting at his desk with his collar unbuttoned, and it had a small circle of five stars on it. We shook hands. He asked me, "What was your mission here?"

This is what they did with visiting experts. I'm not sure how interested he was, and of course I didn't go into any details. I just explained what I had done, and what I concluded.

He listened intently and asked a few questions. I knew this wasn't his primary interest in life. Given what else was going on at the time, I was pleased that the general was showing the level of interest that he did. He thanked me, and I was dismissed. The meeting lasted maybe five minutes.

My conclusions were really pretty simple. The retirement age for high officials was too low. It ought to be raised to 50 immediately and then gradually ratcheted up to 60. It ought to apply evenly and fairly to everybody, regardless of their occupation or status. That includes pension benefits and disability benefits. Some of these changes eventually were put into effect.

My report was 139 pages, and I gave it to Maj. Gen. Courtney Whitney, who was MacArthur's man for revamping the Japanese government.

The date: December 7, 1950.

Other U.S. Missions

There were other technical missions and assignments for the U.S. government over the years. One still continuing is for the State Department in connection with the International Fisheries Commissions Pension Society, which oversees a pension plan for six Canadian-U.S. commissions with a total of about 110 employees. The Society is a Canadian corporation, and every other year I am its president (without pay).

The Japanese assignment was but one of several missions I did for the Department of Defense in connection with benefit plans for its local workers. One was to West Germany, where Rudy and I lived in the visiting-general's house, which came complete with a household staff of several sergeants to take care of us.

Other assignments were to Okinawa, Bermuda, and Goose Bay Airport in Canada.

AID Project

The Agency for International Development decided in the 1950's that it needed a manual to tell the staffs in various countries what social security was all about, what types of systems there were throughout the world, what problems there could be, and how the assets of such systems were invested.

AID told me to travel, to go to selected developing countries, examine their systems, and write the manual from that standpoint. I had two trips. One was to the Middle East and one was to Asia. In the Middle East I went to Greece, Turkey, Egypt, and Lebanon, with maybe a week or so in each country. Of course, I had been to Greece before, so I was sort of familiar with what they'd done. I just wanted to see what had happened subsequently.

The Asian trip was to Sri Lanka (then Ceylon) and the Philippines.

The manual covered general principles of social security in developing countries. How do you cover workers in a country where they're not used to reporting to the government and paying taxes? It was a very elementary manual, meant for people who would be working on the economies in these countries and would want to know about the social security aspect of them.

One thing that the Social Security Administration has done for years is to put out a book that describes, on two pages, the social security system of every country in the world, so I knew something about these systems in advance and would go to see if they performed as advertised.

It's hard to say whether these were good systems or bad ones. The Greek system, for example, had its problems, but it paid benefits. For the people on the receiving end, that was good. There's no such thing as a perfect system. There's also no utterly bad system. It's all a matter of their degrees of effectiveness.

Most of them are modeled after the European systems, and many of these countries set up their systems with the assistance of the ILO, which tried to perpetuate the European type. Such systems are a lot like ours, and while there's no one strict European model, they do share some characteristics. Many of the systems have different retirement ages for men and women. Many systems didn't keep lifetime earnings records. They just looked at the guy's final salary, in his last three years or so, which doesn't lead to a good system.

It's understandable why they didn't want to keep lifetime records. In the old days, this would have to be done by hand, and it was a lot of trouble. It took a lot of people and required a great deal of organization. Of course, today the computer has taken care of much of that.

But all this record-keeping was a hassle with a point. The alternative, which is the European system, encourages — or at least allows — cheating. If the government is only going to look at the last three years of a fellow's salary history, it would be possible for this fellow and the boss to conspire to inflate the salary. It's just a few numbers on a piece of paper. It doesn't cost the boss anything much. The employee may shell out a little more in taxes during those final years but can reap great rewards in pension benefits upon retirement.

It also gives people an incentive to understate their earnings early in their careers. What's the point of the employer and employee paying fully into the system for 40 years, when it's only the last three years that really count? Of course, this kind of cheating is a bit of a gamble. If you die young, your survivors may curse you because their benefits are a pittance. The same is true if you're unlucky enough to become disabled.

That's one of the current problems in the Eastern European countries. They still have that old-style system. The same thing crept into systems in other countries. The old Chilean system was that way. Many of the systems are modeled after that approach, and it's a procedure that can make for poor administration.

Peru and Other Latin American Countries

I went to Peru with Arthur Altmeyer in the early 1950's, after he was forced out of his job as Commissioner *for* Social Security when the Eisenhower Administration took office. (This was done by the long-time Washington trick of eliminating the position — and thus the incumbent — and immediately establishing a new one — in this case, Commissioner *of* Social Security.) He was hired by W.R. Grace & Co. as a consultant because the company had extensive operations in Peru. He was asked to go down there to give advice on the Peruvian social security system to the employer groups.

Although Grace was paying the freight, we actually were traveling at the request of the Peruvian employers association, sort of a national chamber of commerce.

Arthur and I had worked together since the earliest days of Social Security. He was quite knowledgeable about social security and general social security planning. He needed some actuarial help, and he thought my general technical help would be useful, so he asked me to go down there with him. We made a couple of trips there. (Naturally, I took annual leave from my job at the Social Security Administration.)

The problem with Peru was essentially that they had an overly costly system which favored white-collar workers, who were covered by a different and far more generous system than the blue-collar workers. Socially this is backwards. The poor people should have relatively better treatment.

Peru also had an odd system of termination pay. In a nutshell, a worker who retired or got laid off would receive a month's salary for each year of service. This was a payment on top of the pension. This was very costly. The termination-pay and pension systems weren't coordinated at all. The business interests wanted to see them melded into one program that didn't give termination pay but did give better pension benefits.

We spent roughly a week and a half in Peru, delivering a report to the employers association and speaking to members of the government. I don't think we told them anything that they didn't already know, but sometimes they're just waiting for someone from the outside to come in and confirm their theories.

As a result, they brought the two systems much closer together, and Peru scaled back the termination-pay system.

Over the years I worked in a number of other Latin American countries on their social security systems. I acquired a working knowledge of Spanish to be able to read social security material, but my ability to speak or write the language was not as good.

I went to Colombia, Panama, and the Cayman Islands for their governments. Then, just this year, I went to El Salvador for the Inter-American Development Bank. The Organization of American States sent me to many countries, including Bolivia, Dominican Republic, Honduras, Nicaragua, and Venezuela. Another venture was to Surinam for the Aluminum Company of

America, and the Kaiser Foundation made me part of a team to study a proposal for national health insurance in Barbados.

Cyprus

Cyprus was a divided island — part Greek and part Turkish — with a single social security system. The Agency for International Development sent me there in 1962 to examine the program's financing.

The hostility between Greeks and Turks was evident, and when you went from one side of the island to the other, it was like going through customs. But in the social security headquarters in the capital, Nicosia, there they were, Greek and Turk, working side by side.

It didn't take long to find one other thing that united them. They weren't as interested in my advice as they were in getting some money out of the United States.

They had done some figuring on the system and found that it needed an infusion of cash. Their solution was to ask for a handout. They wanted the United States to fork over millions of dollars in a lump sum. They weren't very specific on the amount, just something with a lot of zeroes and commas. Then they could take the money and invest it. The returns from the investment would float the system.

What an idea! Net cost (to them): $0.

I took one look at the provisions of their program and rendered my advice: If you want a financially sound system, raise contributions. In that way you don't need us.

I don't think that was what they wanted to hear.

Before leaving the island, I gave a talk to union officials about what the U.S. Social Security system was like and how it developed. AID got both Greek and Turkish union officials to come, which at the time was a rare occurrence.

Saudi Arabia

In 1965 Saudi Arabia asked the United States for help with its civil service and military retirement systems. Previously they had been relying on Egypt because that country has always had a number of trained actuaries. But at that time Egyptian President Gamal Abdel Nasser had a falling out with the Saudis. It didn't come to a shooting war, but the two countries were on poor terms. So the Saudis wanted to get rid of any reliance on Egypt, and they came to the United States for this and many other things.

This was an AID project, but it was unusual because the Saudis offered to pay for the help. It was only right, and they had the money. They paid for my travel and reimbursed the U.S. government for my salary.

I went over there alone at first for about a week to see what the system was like and to ask for data. In Saudi Arabia it was more than just an appraisal; I was going to make a real valuation.

The military retirement system wasn't going to be easy to evaluate because some of the information that I needed was, naturally, a state secret. Information on the number of active military personnel and their ages was classified. I could find out all sorts of information about the pensioners on the rolls, though. Also, I could get bottom-line figures on how much money was being paid out, how much was being collected, and what the military pay scales were.

This was batting partially blind, but they obviously must have liked my work because they subsequently asked me to come back at three-year intervals until just recently. By their law every three years they had to have a valuation of their two systems.

As she's done on many of my other trips, Rudy accompanied me not only as my wife, but also as my secretary. The time she spent in Saudi Arabia was a shock because of the severe restrictions placed on women there. She couldn't go with me to the office, so she was pretty much marooned at the hotel. They sent over a typewriter for her to do her job. On one occasion, they bought her a brand new IBM like the one she was used to at home, and a new table and chair.

She could go around the hotel by herself, but she couldn't go out of the building alone. The first time that she went there it really got to her. Three weeks cooped up in a hotel made her kind of emotional. On later trips she knew what to expect, so she didn't let it bother her as much.

On one of our trips there was a cholera epidemic, and they thought we ought to get shots. They were giving injections at the office, so they sent a car for Rudy to come over for that. They whisked her in to see the doctor and whisked her out. I don't know if she was there long enough even to say "ow."

There were a couple of things about the Saudi system that were rather unique, and they're more of a cultural thing than anything else. One was that when they paid survivor benefits for a person who had died, the male children got much more than the female children. This was the case in the early days I was there and for a few years after that. The system very definitely discriminated against females. The survivor benefits paid to male children were often higher than those paid to the widow.

Of course I was judicious enough not to say, "Look, you guys, this just isn't right." But when they'd ask what was done in other systems, I'd point out that in other countries they didn't do things this way. I didn't tell them that they were wrong or barbaric. I just pointed out the situation elsewhere.

They no longer have such provisions and haven't for some years. They have completely equal treatment. The male orphan gets the same as the female orphan. I don't know whether the change was due to what I told them. They would, of course, have gotten the same answer from virtually anybody they asked.

The other thing that's interesting about these Saudi systems is that, unlike in many countries, they have piled up a lot of money because the government never has been poor. Generally the contribution rate was something like 9 percent from the employee and 9 to 13 percent from the employer.

For years, the Saudis invested the money in a very good portfolio of foreign stocks, heavily into blue chips on the New York Stock Exchange. They also had an assortment of U.S. and foreign bonds and other securities. They were a little bit unsophisticated in the area of finance because when the market dropped, and the stocks weren't worth what they'd paid for them, they were quite dismayed. They realized that the stocks could go up in value, but they were shocked to learn that the opposite was also true. As a result, they ceased investing in foreign stocks.

The Saudis were good businessmen who labored under certain religious restrictions. The Koran, for example, said that it was a sin to charge interest. So how does a good follower of Islam behave in the bond market? Well, the money you get isn't interest, that's how. It's a reward that you are given for the use of your money. We all know that's what interest is, but as long as they didn't call it that, they were OK.

When I went there the last time, they decided, quite rightly, that I wasn't going to live forever, so they ought to get another actuary. They explained it to me and were very nice when they did it. Not that I was slipping to any extent that they could see, but they thought it would be desirable to get an actuarial firm rather than one person. They asked me to help them, and I did by writing the letter for them to outline the specifications of the job which needed to be done.

I also gave them the names of some firms, one in Germany, a couple in Great Britain, and a couple in the United States. About the time they got the letters sent out, there was trouble in Kuwait, and they had trouble getting people to come over there to bid on the work. For one thing it was starting to look like war, and for another thing, the Saudis weren't going to pay their expenses. Then too, the Saudis had more important matters on their minds.

Bermuda

I started going there in the early 1970's. A friend of mine, an actuary named Laurie Longley-Cook, was in Bermuda because there is a fair amount of insurance run from there. The offshore insurance companies are there because it is a very stable government.

This fellow was on their hospital insurance board. They have a hospital insurance system there which is something like Medicare, but it applies to the whole population, except children (who are given "free" care, paid for out of general revenues). It is a form of national health insurance. It's a fairly simple system, though, because they only have one hospital in Bermuda. It has two branches, a general hospital and a mental hospital. One complexity about this program that creates actuarial problems is that most of the persons are covered by buying the basic protection from an insurance company or an employer's "approved scheme," all at the standard premium rate which I develop.

They establish premium rates that people have to pay and the employer matches. Each year they have to determine the rates that are going to be charged, and there's usually a new feature or two added over the course of the year as the hospitals offer more services, such as putting in a dialysis unit or a CAT scanner.

The insurance system also covers people who have to go abroad for treatment. Bermuda is a place of about 60,000 people, and the hospital there can't have all the facilities that a big hospital in the United States has.

They needed an actuary to establish the rates for this system, and my friend, having been appointed to the board of the hospital insurance system, could no longer do it. He recommended that they have me do it.

I get to go down there for four or five days every winter to raise their premium rates to an adequate level. It's not a hard job, although there is a fair amount of intensive work. And it's one of the most pleasant places on Earth. Well, somebody has to take these hardship assignments.

Trust Territory of the Pacific Islands
(Micronesia)

This is a group of islands out in the Central Pacific, in area, including the ocean between them, that is as big as the United States. It floats off in mid-ocean, north of New Guinea, east of the Philippines, south of Japan and west of Hawaii. It has a population of 150,000 or so.

The United States was the trustee for the Territory, appointed by the United Nations. During the years the United States had been criticized for its stewardship, and one of these complaints was that there was no social security system for the people there.

The Department of Interior asked me to go out there in the mid-1960's, survey the situation, and develop a social security system. I went out and set up the system, which began operations in 1967. In addition to the social security system, I also established a system of prior service benefits, providing pensions for people there who had worked in the past for the U.S. government.

I went back every now and then to make an actuarial valuation of how the system was doing. Like any other social security system, from time to time there are people wanting to change it, such as raising the benefits when inflation occurred. When I left the government in 1970, I continued this work.

Just a few years ago the end of the trusteeship came, and the various constituent parts of it voted on what to do. They could become independent nations, they could become part of the United States, or they could be sort of associated with the United States.

The Northern Marianas voted to become part of the United States, and they are now a U.S. territory the same as Guam and Puerto Rico. They in essence came under the U.S. Social Security system. People who work there are covered by Social Security just like people who work in Topeka.

The trust territory was administered from Saipan, Northern Mariana Islands, and that's where I worked. The first time I went there, they had me go to some of the other islands to get a feel for what they were like. Saipan, for example, is more developed than the other islands.

The other three portions of the Territory voted to become independent nations but sort of under the protectorate of the United States. They are the Marshall Islands, Palau, and the Federated States of Micronesia. Therefore the social security system there was essentially divided up into four parts.

Africa and Asia

As long as I'm mentioning exotic travel, these come to mind. My work in these parts of the world wasn't for the government. For years I had been associated with the pension plans of the Lutheran Church in America. For the most part I did this *pro bono*, although I did serve for pay seven months in 1987 as president of the LCA Board of Pensions.

Rudy and I traveled to India, Malaysia, and several nations in Africa, including Cameroun, Ethiopia, Liberia, Namibia,

Nigeria, and Tanzania to help with the church pension plans there. The plans are small, and so are the pensions. But nobody is doing this work for the money. We often would live with the missionaries under sometimes primitive conditions. It was not unusual for hospitals to be unsanitary, water to need boiling, lights to flicker out for no apparent reason, or governments to be headed by bigoted or homicidal flakes.

These church people live and work with dedication and good cheer. I was glad to have made whatever contribution I could toward helping them have a more secure retirement.

Chile

This country led the way for social security in the Western Hemisphere in the 1920's, and there are some who say it's doing the same for the world right now. The system in Chile was privatized in 1981, and other countries, including Argentina, Brazil, Mexico, and the nations of Eastern Europe, are looking at it as they reconsider their own programs.

Chile had a fragmented and inequitable system based on the European model but got rid of it in favor of a new one. Everybody with the exception of the military is covered by it. The program was a radical departure from the past and perhaps could not have been done without a military dictatorship.

After years of mismanagement, Chile's old system just sank deeper and deeper into trouble. It had poor administration and poor compliance with the law. Its investments went up in smoke because of the country's horrible inflation, and the government didn't put the money into the system that it was supposed to.

Chile's dictator, Augusto Pinochet, declared that they were going to have a completely new system. Instead of having the employer pay most of the cost, the government pay some of the cost, and the worker pay a small part of the cost, now the entire cost is borne by the worker. The theory was that this would help business because it would lower labor costs. That was a myth because at the same time that it did this, the Pinochet government said there would be an 18 percent increase in every salary in the country.

The system works in much the same way that individual retirement accounts, or IRA's, operate in this country. A dozen or so private pension companies administer it. The worker is taxed 10 percent, and that money is invested by whatever pension company is handling the individual's account. Three times a year, the worker receives a financial statement, showing how much money has been socked away and how the investments are doing.

Many people in this country say that we ought to privatize the U.S. system. They say that everybody ought to take care of themselves, that we all ought to have IRA's, and none of this social welfare.

What they don't realize about the Chilean system is that the government puts an awful lot of money into it because of two elements. First, they put up money to pay for people's past service. When they retire under the new system, the government puts up a huge sum of money for each person, representing more or less the actuarial value of the benefits which they accrued under the old system. Second, they guarantee a very high minimum pension. If the IRA account plus the past service credit doesn't bring a pension up to roughly 40 percent of the average wage in the country, which is a very high amount (that's what a U.S. average-wage worker gets under Social Security), the government will put in money in a lump sum to build the pension up to this level.

In 1984 I was invited by the association of pension insurance companies to come to Chile and study their new plan. I went down there with the belief that I would say it's a bad idea because I'm so opposed to the people in this country who want to privatize Social Security. But when I examined the situation in Chile, I concluded that what they had done was good. It may not have been the only way that they could have remedied the situation, but it certainly was successful. However, I still think that for the United States it would be terrible.

Why do I think it's a good idea for Chile?

It's working, and it's hard to argue with that. It's the only system like this in the world. They're getting pretty good coverage compliance. I think that the covered people are reasonably satisfied and reassured because they get frequent financial reports on their retirement accounts. This is something that brings popular support. The old system had been so poorly administered that the people had lost confidence in it.

This new system is run on the basis of an indexed currency. In other words, it's tied to the inflation rate and will tend to maintain its purchasing power over time. The pension companies operate the funds by buying investments, most of which are indexed. For example, debt instruments of the Central Bank and government bonds are indexed. Thus, inflation is built into the system.

There are various options upon retirement. The payout is based on how much money you put into the fund. The individual can then take that money and buy a lifetime annuity, or draw it down like an IRA.

Now let's look at the other side of the coin, the bad side, because nothing's perfect in this world. I didn't just go down there and butter them up and say this is a great system.

A lot of the money that they're investing — 50 percent of their assets — is in government bonds or debt instruments of the Central Bank. These investments pay a pretty good rate of interest, but it's really money going around in a circle just like our money does in the Social Security trust funds.

Also, as I mentioned earlier, the government is paying huge sums of money for past service and for building minimum pensions, and it will continue to do this for many years. Where does the government get that money? It borrows. You could make the argument that the government is borrowing it from the pension insurance companies that are investing in government bonds and Central Bank obligations.

It is also the government's belief that the 10 percent contribution rate, along with earnings from the funds' investments over time, will build up sufficiently so that in the long run they'll pay quite adequate pensions, such as 70 percent of salary.

This is based on the hope that they'll get 7 percent to 8 percent real interest, which is interest after inflation. It's been true in the last 10 years that they've done this well — and even better. But over the long run most financial people, economists and actuaries say that you can't get real interest that high forever. The economies just won't bear it. Our real interest rates here in the United States are 2 percent or 3 percent a year. In a system like Chile's it makes a real difference if the investments are earning 8 percent or 3 percent real interest a year.

Overall, though, it's a good system. It works in Chile, at least for now.

CHAPTER NINE

IT WILL OUTLIVE US ALL

I guess if I wanted to sell a million copies of this book, I'd have to tell you that Social Security is a lousy deal, that it's run by a bunch of stumblebums, and that it's going to leave you living in a refrigerator carton making soup out of a boiled shoe when you retire.

Sorry!

This may hit you as painfully dull, but the program works. It is not headed for calamity because our political system will not let that happen.

There are creepy organizations out there trying to scare people into sending them money so they can go about the job of "saving" Social Security.

I am here to tell you that these outfits have had a negligible effect — if any — on the course of Social Security. I have been aghast at the way people have exaggerated Social Security's pitfalls. It undermines public confidence and just gets people to waste their money.

Not too long ago I came across a flyer from the publisher of one of these alarmist books, this one written by a former Social Security commissioner, Dorcas Hardy [8]. The publisher's flyer, which was meant to hook people's attention, started off with a bang: ''The Social Security system is doomed.''

And the book itself states, ''The Social Security system is a ticking time bomb. In the next century, just a few years away, the United States will face a potentially devastating crisis: The retirement check that should be sent to benefit millions of Americans will not be there.''

Hogwash.

Ms. Hardy, who was Commissioner of Social Security from 1986 to 1989, knows better, or at least she ought to. By the way, the situation which she now finds so alarming existed while she was in office, but she neglected to say anything about it then.

This alarmism, which I'm convinced is a cynical and shameful attempt to gin up some money and publicity by selling a few warped books, is rooted in a deliberately narrow view of the official actuarial estimates and purposefully fails to take into account human nature and political reality.

As I have said earlier, actuarial estimates sort of fire a shotgun at the future, and the truth often lies somewhere around the middle of the pattern. These middle-of-the-road estimates for the future may be too optimistic or too pessimistic, but they're as good a stab at this as any. The figures show that the system will have no problem paying benefits until the year 2036.

But let's assume I'm wrong. What will happen? We can look to very recent history for the answer. Social Security unquestionably was headed for disaster in the early 1980's, and it was saved.

That action concentrated on the short-range financing problems of the system. Although it did address some of the long-range concerns, it must be remembered that this was done in a big hurry, so some fine-tuning will be necessary in the future. Overall, though, the system is sound for years to come.

President Reagan reflected on this at the 1983 ceremony when he signed the rescue bill into law:

"This bill demonstrates for all time our nation's commitment to Social Security. It assures the elderly that America will always keep the promises made in troubled times a half century ago. It assures those who are still working that they, too, have a pact with the future. From this day forward, they have our pledge that they will get their fair share of benefits when they retire."

He went on to say that the bill was "a clear and dramatic demonstration that our system can work when men and women of good will join together to make it work."

Three years later, Reagan was still bullish on Social Security when he addressed a group of students by television "The Social Security system is solvent enough to assure these students of benefits when they become senior citizens," he said.

The system may be somewhat different many years from now, but its general characteristics will be much the same as they are now.

The adjustments that will be needed to keep the system in balance in the future are not radical. An upward nudge in the retirement age and maybe moving taxes up a little will be all that's needed to avert a problem that probably won't come up for another 40 years, even if nothing is done.

American seniors are, by and large, not selfish and concerned only with themselves. If it were true that the Social Security program would operate successfully for their lifetimes but then would collapse, American seniors would be concerned about such a horrendous situation for their sake of their children and grandchildren.

Ms. Hardy's book, *Social Insecurity: The Crisis in America's Social Security System and How to Plan Now for Your Own Financial Survival*, contains a lot of half-truths and outright factual errors. It's a sloppy piece of work. For example, she writes that under current law the Social Security trust fund will build up to a peak of $12 trillion in 2030. But the 1991 Trustees Report, which she cites elsewhere in her book, puts that figure at $8 trillion.

One of the half-truths is that the Social Security trust fund surpluses are shuffled around in a "shell game" to pay for other government operations. In truth, this money is invested in government bonds, the same bonds that are bought by mutual funds, banks, and individuals. It's an investment, and it pays a fair rate of interest.

The fact that the money isn't lying around in an account somewhere shouldn't alarm anybody. Banks, for example, don't take your money and throw it in the back of the vault. It is "spent" — that is, loaned out — as fast as the bank can find a suitable borrower.

The bonds held by the trust funds — as well as the interest paid on them — are just as valid as are all other government bonds. They are backed by the full faith and credit of the United States. That means something, even when the government is borrowing money from itself.

This touches on a problem, though. Not only is the trust fund being used to finance part of the government's budget deficit, it is used to mask the true size of the deficit — through bookkeeping tricks that only politicians can dream up and get away with.

The reason is that the fund is now building up rapidly and will soon be too large. Pat Moynihan, for one, wants to drop this fig leaf. He wants to cut the payroll tax to the point where the system doesn't build up so greatly but only takes in as much as it currently needs, which is a pay-as-you-go system. Such a financing procedure is efficient and honest.

As you may have guessed, I am strongly in favor of that and have testified on behalf of the Moynihan proposal numerous times before congressional committees. (And Pat is so kind as to say that I had suggested this approach to him in earlier testimony.) Even though this is a tax cut, it doesn't have a lot of friends in Congress or the Administration. Moynihan hasn't been able to get it through the Senate, but he keeps bringing it back every time that it dies. One day, a sufficient number of his colleagues may see the light.

But the financing of Social Security still causes some anxiety even among those who do not worry about system going up in smoke before they can draw benefits.

It is said by some that a lot of people pay more Social Security taxes than income taxes, and therefore it's a horrible system and it's too expensive. That viewpoint has a lot of fallacies.

Take, for example, a kid who goes to work in an ice cream store and earns a couple hundred dollars. There's no income tax on that money, but the kid and his employer pay the Social Security tax.

So what's the problem with that?

That doesn't seem to be a bad situation. There's no relationship between the two taxes. With Social Security, people are essentially buying retirement, survivor, and disability insurance. With income tax, they're just paying taxes.

If you look at people in full-time jobs, they may or may not pay more Social Security tax than income tax. If they're low-income they won't pay much income tax, but everybody should pay their fair share of Social Security.

Consider another example. A fellow earns $14,000 a year, and he has a wife and child. He's paying more Social Security tax than income tax. Part of the reason is that someone in his income range qualifies for an earned income credit, which reduces his income tax to help him afford the Social Security tax, which comes to about $1,071 a year.

People's attitudes toward Social Security have changed over the last 20 years or so. I think that people generally, regardless of age, will say that Social Security has been a fine thing. The younger people will say that it has helped their parents and made the difference between their having a miserable life or getting along alright. It has saved the young from the burden of having to support their parents.

But younger people don't have confidence that the system's going to be there when they retire. Twenty years ago or earlier, there was little lack of confidence in the system. That confidence was shaken by the two major crises in Social Security in 1977 and the early 1980's, even though the system averted financial collapse then. Some of that confidence has since come back, but it ought to be higher.

The American Council of Life Insurance conducts an annual survey on public attitudes toward life insurance in general. One additional topic in the survey has always been to measure people's confidence in the future of Social Security. Public opinion polls are sometimes deceptive or inconclusive, However, in this case, when the same question is asked year after year, the trends that show up are significant.

In 1975, 63 percent of the people polled were confident in the future of the Social Security system. That figure dropped in the 1970's as the program developed financing problems and reached a trough of 34 percent in 1984 and 1985. Since then, the confidence level has increased and was 54 percent in 1990 and

1991. That is not too impressive a figure, but at least it is encouraging that confidence has been increasing.

When we view the situation by age, it is not surprising that the confidence level among younger persons is around 40 percent. By contrast, people aged 65 and over have a 75 percent confidence level in the system. Whether the figure is higher for people over 65 because of their maturity and their breadth of knowledge, or whether it is merely because they know that, for the next 10 or 15 years, there are no problems, I would not want to say. It may be because those over age 65 considered the matter more fully and understand the situation better.

The fund now has some $325 billion in it, and by the end of the century it will be almost $1 trillion. That's a fair sum of money in anybody's league. All the estimates show that it won't have any financial problems for at least 25 years, and perhaps much longer.

As the Baby Boom generation hits retirement age, beginning in 2010, the trust-fund balance will begin to increase much less rapidly and will reach a peak about 30 years from now. Then it will begin falling rapidly, and within 10 to 15 years after that, it will be exhausted. This is a "roller-coaster" kind of financing, in which a huge fund is built up and then goes rapidly downhill. That can cause all sorts of problems in the economy.

Building up a large trust fund and then depleting it is not a sensible means of financing any continuing pension plan. In a private plan, it is necessary to build up reserves because the employer might go out of business. This gives some guarantee to the participants and the pensioners that the promised benefits will be paid. In a national program, this is not necessary. It can be taken for granted that the national government will go on into perpetuity.

This is my argument for pay-as-you-go financing, which is the way the system was bankrolled in the 1960's and early 1970's.

It would maintain a trust-fund balance equal to about what would have to be paid out in benefits for a year. This would cushion the system against economic shocks and give breathing room to political leaders who might have to step in sometime in the future to make adjustments. It would maintain the system on a constantly solid footing, instead of the current financing scheme that either has the program awash in money or falling into the abyss.

This plays into the hands of people who want to sell books, and it helps to keep people on edge. Some of this is natural. The public is always skeptical of the government, especially in recent years.

But there is no doubt in my mind that Social Security will be here in its present relative form as long as the United States exists. The dollars will be different, and the retirement ages may be different. However, those changes will be driven by the economy, inflation, and health advances that extend life expectancy.

There is another complaint from the young, though. They believe that, even if Social Security is around when they retire, they won't live long enough to get back all the money they paid in taxes.

Some of them are right. That's how the system is supposed to work. Some people get back more than they paid in, and some people get back less. There are two aspects to Social Security; one is the "social" feature, taking money from the pockets of the well-to-do and putting it in the pockets of the needy. The other aspect is security. This is the nature of insurance. We pay for insurance protection on our homes, our cars, and our lives. If the house doesn't burn down, the car doesn't get wrecked, or we don't die, the insurance company doesn't pay any money, and what we paid in premiums we don't get back.

Consider the hypothetical case of two workers who have been employed at the same salaries for their entire careers and have been paying Social Security taxes all that time. One dies at his desk on his 65th birthday and leaves no eligible survivors. He paid all that money in for all those years and got nothing back. Not a dime.

But the other guy retires at 65 and lives to be 100. He will get back far more than he paid in, even after you compute the interest he could have collected on the money that was taken from him by the payroll tax. He got a good deal.

These are individual cases. If we project this to a national scale, we get a better view of how the system works.

Take the people who are now 20 years old. Roughly 80 percent of them can expect to be alive on their 65th birthday, and they will then live beyond that, *on the average,* for 18 years. That means some of them may die the next day, while others live another 35 years or even longer.

All of them collect something. Even the 25 percent who died before retiring got something for their money. Their surviving spouses and dependents are eligible to collect, and on top of that during their working lives they were insured against the calamity of becoming disabled.

As it happens, just by chance, the highly-paid young worker just about breaks even, on the average, taking into account the value of money over time. But that's based only on the taxes he or she has paid for the retirement aspect of Social Security.

In a way, this is only looking at part of the picture. The amount of money paid into the system by the employee is matched by the employer, and in the case of the self-employed the individual's contribution is double because this person pays both shares of the Social Security tax.

But it is incorrect to consider the employer's share of the tax as something that ought to be payable to the individual. This is like other payroll-related costs that an employer bears, such as health insurance and pension funds. Not everybody will get back what the employer has paid on their behalf. It is this pooling of funds and spreading of risk that makes these plans affordable and workable.

Also, if there were no Social Security program, there is no assurance that the employer would pay that money to the employee as added salary or benefits. It is conceivable (and perhaps more likely) that if there were no Social Security program, the employer might lower prices instead of raising salaries.

This argument is a bit harder for the self-employed to accept, but the broad social principles at work in a place the size of General Motors also apply to the one-person shop.

If you put the system on a strictly individual-equity basis, so that everybody got exactly what they paid for, nothing more and nothing less, then the young, higher paid would make out better than they do under the current system (assuming that they would receive what their employer now pays in Social Security taxes).

But if we did that, what would we do about the people with lower incomes? Sometimes the answer comes back that the government should take care of them. Well, that's fine, but the government isn't somebody else; it's us. If the government has to pay for something, it taxes us. It makes no difference, in the final analysis, whether it's an income tax or a Social Security tax.

The system is more than equitable to the people with low incomes. A person who has held a minimum-wage job for a lifetime will get back far, far more in retirement than was paid into the system by the employee and the employer. It's not equitable, but it's fair. The alternative would be to pay them benefits that were so low as to not be meaningful, and these people would then have to supplement that by drawing money from elsewhere in order to survive. That money would likely come from the public welfare system. Guess who pays for that.

Social Security will endure because it is so large, and so much a part of our national machinery, that it just cannot be stopped.

Medicare is a different story. I am not predicting Medicare's collapse, nor advocating its demise. However, it's possible, and even likely, that Medicare will be replaced sometime in the future by some form of national health insurance.

Let me digress a moment to discuss Medicare's financing problems, both past and future. First of all, neither branch of Medicare — Hospital Insurance (Part A) and Supplementary Medical Insurance (Part B, mainly for doctor bills) — has ever had a financial crisis as Social Security had in the early 1980's, and to a lesser extent in the late 1970's.

True, tax rates for hospital insurance had to be increased several times over what was originally scheduled, and now the trust fund is estimated to go belly up in about 10 years (possibly even in eight years). The originally scheduled combined employer-employee rate for the long run was 1.6 percent. If the long-term disability beneficiaries had been included (as they were in legislation in 1972), the rate would have been 1.8 percent. Current law provides a rate of 2.9 percent for all future years, or, in relative terms, 61 percent higher than originally scheduled. (Not such a great estimate was made at the inception of Medicare!) Furthermore, the best estimate of the rate over the long run (some 50 years hence) is about 10 percent. Cost trouble certainly lies ahead for Medicare, unlike the situation for Social Security.

It is also true that the Part B premium rate from the enrolee and the government combined has soared. Originally, in 1966, this rate was $6 a month, shared equally. In 1992 it is $121.60, payable 26 percent by the enrollee and 74 percent by the government (that's you if you're a taxpayer). But Part B is on a one-year term insurance basis, so the premium rates can be — and have been — changed annually, and this keeps the system fiscally sound. However, whether it is affordable or cost effective may be a different matter.

There are various forms of national health insurance. At one extreme is what they had in the Soviet Union, where all the doctors were on the government payroll, hospitals all belonged to the government, and all drugs were made by the government. People directly paid either nothing or very little for it; instead it was paid for by general taxes.

Then there is the British system, in which all of the doctors have some degree of independence but are still much under the control of the government. They get paid a monthly capitation fee, not fees for each service. Then there is the Canadian approach under which the doctors continue to work as they always have, but the fees are tightly controlled by the government. People directly pay very little or nothing for their medical services.

I'm not enthusiastic about it, but I think that we're going to move to something in the general area of national health insurance. We've gotten ourselves into a bad position, where everybody's so antagonistic with each other. The doctors think the government's against them, the insurance companies are against them, the employers are against them, and even their patients are against them. The patients may think their own doctors are fine, but the rest of the medical profession is a bunch of money grubbers who gouge the sick.

The profit motive sometimes does not serve us well here. If you tighten up on Medicare fees, the doctors and the hospitals are going to find other ways to generate the money they think they should be getting. One way is to charge non-Medicare patients more, in essence shifting the costs to them. Another is to perform more services of dubious necessity.

All this raises the big question of how much health care do people really need. Should they all be treated like the President of the United States or very rich people who have a doctor on call all the time? Well, you can't do that for everybody. Or do you have restrictions as they do in England, where certain operations, such as kidney transplants, won't be done for people over a certain age?

On top of the moral and ethical questions is the fact that people just don't want to pay for some things. I would like to have a greatly expanded Medicaid program so that people who are poor can get necessary medical attention, and the doctors and hospitals can be paid fairly for their services. One of the troubles with Medicaid now is that doctors don't want to deal with it because the fees set by the system are far too low. Hospitals and nursing homes feel the same way. The solution, of course, would be to raise the limits on how much Medicaid will pay, but that would mean higher taxes to finance it. And people do not want to pay more taxes.

I don't think custodial nursing home care is an insurable risk. If you make it available as a right, it will be overused, although not by people with lots of money. Nursing homes are not the nicest places in the world to live. But people in the lower economic strata would live much better in nursing homes (which meet government standards) than they have otherwise. When they get to be old and in somewhat ill health, a nursing home would be a step up in their living conditions, and they'd be quite willing to go. It is hard, for example, for a government system to determine whether a person is disabled and thus entitled to monthly benefits. Sorting out who should go to a nursing home, and who should not, is even more difficult.

This process, to put it bluntly, is to figure out who's malingering and who really needs help. Tests for this are subjective at best. The need for custodial-nursing-home benefits is generally measured by the inability to perform a certain number of so-called activities of daily living. These activities include feeding oneself, dressing, getting in and out of bed, and going to the bathroom. With a little coaching and effort, one can flunk any of these tests.

It's sort of like determining disability, something that has caused the Social Security system fits since it became part of the program in 1956. Suppose some guy says he can't work because his back hurts. Medical tests don't show anything, but the fellow insists the pain is excruciating. Do you proceed on the basis of his complaint alone, or do you base your judgment on the medical tests, which say that his back is just fine? On the one hand he might be faking (people do that, you know), but on the other hand the tests might be wrong or might have missed something.

It sounds very cruel, but as an actuary you have to look at the possibility of malingering. I'm convinced that custodial nursing home care is just not possible under social insurance. I'm strongly in favor of social insurance to cover risks where it can work.

So that still leaves us with the problem of what to do about nursing home care. It's expensive, but lots of people really need it — and over the long-run future, as our population ages, many more will need it. I would provide it under Medicaid but not the way it's done now.

Medicaid forces the elderly to go through the humiliation of making themselves poor in order to qualify for the nursing home benefits. Many people are finding a way around this by disposing of their assets, often by giving them to their children.

Even then, the patient has to find a nursing home that accepts Medicaid. Often such homes set aside just a certain number of beds for Medicaid patients. Even if they otherwise have room, they won't accept more Medicaid patients because they can't afford the loss. Medicaid's fees are just too low.

I would liberalize Medicaid greatly. I would not make people spend down their resources or use all their income.

Instead, I would put a lien on their resources. Let them keep their houses, bank accounts, investments, and much of their income. This would remain in effect as long as the individual or the spouse were alive. But once the last one had died, the government could lay claim to part or all of the estate to recover the costs of nursing home care. The effect of this would be to wipe out some inheritances, but I'm not a big believer in inherited wealth anyway.

The net result is still going to be money out of the government's pocket — lots of it. It's going to mean higher taxes to pay for it. But I believe that this is something that rightfully falls on society, and if we all have to chip in to pay for it, then we do. I'm willing to pay more taxes to see that poor people in the country get more medical care.

That's off in the future, however.

So nearly a half century after the death of Franklin D. Roosevelt, the Social Security system still has not achieved the cradle-to-grave protection that its founders wanted. Nevertheless, the system that we have now is a testimony to their political wisdom and foresight, and to the responsible actions of those who have followed them.

FDR was, without a doubt, a political genius, who was interested in doing good things for the country. His gut told him that once this system got started, the nation's economy and the expectations of its people would mold themselves around it. Everyone would have a stake in it. Employers base their pension plans on it, and workers plan for their retirement with it.

Social Security is fair to society, and we can be secure in the knowledge that it will outlive us all.

ILLUSTRATIONS

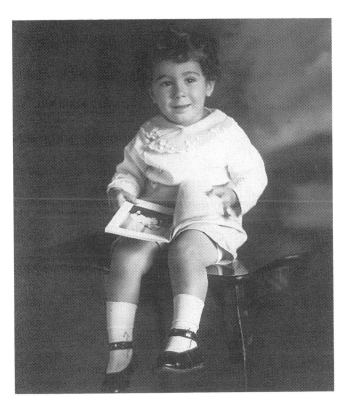

Robert J. Myers, circa 1915.

The boyhood home of Robert J. Myers in Elkins Park, Pennsylvania. The house was built by maternal grandfather Julius Hirsh, and remained in the family until just recently.

Bob Myers traveling in Germany in 1931, with Grandmother Sarah Hirsh.

Rudy Myers in 1941, aboard the American Bantam.

Rudy and Bob Myers in Egypt in 1961. Bob was on a mission for the Agency for International Development, examining social security systems in developing nations.

Examining the government bonds bought by the Social Security trust funds in 1968. Front row: Labor Secretary W. Willard Wirtz, Treasury Secretary Henry H. Fowler, HEW Acting Secretary Wilbur J. Cohen. Back row: Social Security Commissioner Robert M. Ball, Social Security Chief Actuary Robert J. Myers.

Treasury Department Photo

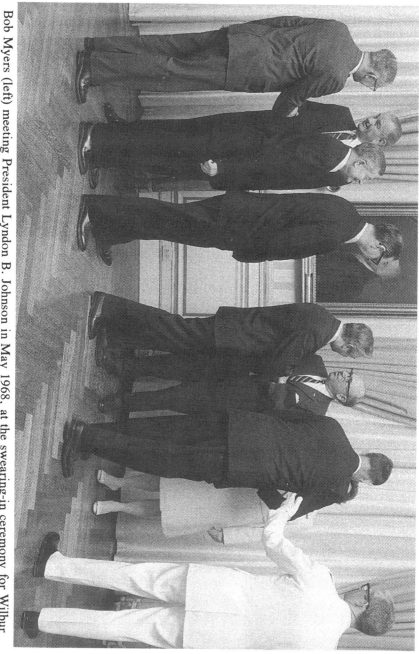

Bob Myers (left) meeting President Lyndon B. Johnson in May 1968, at the swearing-in ceremony for Wilbur Cohen (sixth from left) as Secretary of Health, Education, and Welfare.

White House Photo

Rudy and Bob Myers greeting Japanese Crown Prince (now Emperor) Akahito in 1976, at a meeting of the International Congress of Actuaries. Bob was Vice President of the International Actuarial Association at the time.

The Myers Family in December 1988: Rudy, Jonathan, Eric, and Bob

PUBLICATIONS

[Editor's Note: Beginning with "An Upper Limit for the Roots of an Equation," published in *American Mathematical Monthly* in January 1933, Robert J. Myers has authored (or co-authored) nearly 900 books, articles, and technical reports. The complete list is far too lengthy to reproduce here. We have selected the following publications, classified as "popular" or "technical," as representing his major contributions to the published literature.]

Popular Publications

1. "War and Postwar Experience in Regard to the Sex Ratio at Birth in Various Countries," *Human Biology*, December 1949.

2. "Life Insurance in Japan," *The Spectator*, May 1951. (Reprinted in *The South African Insurance Magazine*, August 1951.)

3.   "The First U.S. Government Actuary and His Successors," *Transactions of the Society of Actuaries*, VII (1955).

4.   "Economic Security in the Soviet Union," *Transactions of the Society of Actuaries*, XI (1959).

5.   "Forty Years of Actuarial Responsibilities in the U.S. Social Security Program," *Transactions of the Society of Actuaries*, XXVII (1975).

6.   "Pensions and Sex," *Civil Rights Digest*, Winter 1977.

7.   "Why Do People Retire from Work Early?" *Social Security Bulletin*, September 1982. (Summarized in *Aging and Work*, Vol. 5, No. 2, 1982.)

8.   "The Extent of General Revenue Financing in the Social Security Program as a Result of the 1983 Amendments," *Employee Benefits Journal*, June 1984.

9.   "Social Security: Unfair to Black Americans?" *Business Forum*, Fall 1984.

10. "The Social Security Benefit Notch Problem: What It Is and What It Is Not," *The Generational Journal*, July 1988.

11. "The Future of Medicare and Its Implication for the Private Insurance Industry," *The Generational Journal*, April 1989.

12. "Social Security and the Federal Budget: Some Mirages, Myths, and Solutions," *Journal of the American Society of CLU and ChFC*, March 1988.

13. "The Centenary of the First National Pension Program," *Contingencies*, July/August 1989.

14. "Should the Social Security Age for First Benefits or for Full Benefits Be Changed? Yes, Changes Are Needed," published in *Retirement and Public Policy*, edited by Alicia H. Munnell, National Academy of Social Insurance, January 1990.

15. "Some Kind Words about the Recently Departed Medicare Catastrophic Coverage Program," *Contingencies*, July/August 1990.

16. "The Success of the 1983 Amendments to the Social Security Act in Saving the System," *Benefits Quarterly*, Fourth Quarter, 1990.

17. "Pay-As-You-Go Financing for Social Security Is the Only Way to Go," *Journal of the American Society of CLU and ChFC*, January 1991.

18. "Will Social Security Be There When the Baby-Boomers Retire?" E.J. Faulkner Lecture, University of Nebraska, October 17, 1991.

19. "Can the Government Operate Programs Efficiently and Inexpensively?" *Contingencies*, March/April 1992.

20. "Chile's Social Security Reform, after Ten Years," *Benefits Quarterly*, Third Quarter, 1992.

Technical Publications

1. "Errors and Bias in the Reporting of Ages in Census Data," *Transactions of the Actuarial Society of America*, XLI (1940).

2. "The Effect of Age of Mother and Birth Order on Sex Ratio at Birth," *Milbank Memorial Fund Quarterly*, July 1954.

3. "Effect of Differing Fertility and Mortality Trends on Costs of Social Insurance Programs Providing Old-age Benefits," *Transactions of the Fifteenth International Congress of Actuaries*, Vol. II, October 1957.

4. "The Effect of Dynamic Economic Conditions on a Static-Provision National Pension Scheme," *Transactions of the Seventeenth International Congress of Actuaries*, Vol. III, Part 1, May/June 1964.

5. *Medicare*. Homewood: Richard D. Irwin, Inc., 1970.

6. "Fallacies Expounded by Advocates of National Health Insurance," *New York Medicine,* November 1971.

7. "Is Social Security Really Insurance?" *CLU Journal*, July 1974.

8. *Indexation of Pension and Other Benefits*. Homewood: Richard D. Irwin, Inc., 1978.

9. "Investment Policies and Procedures of the Social Security Trust Funds," *Social Security Bulletin*, January 1982.

10. "United States Life Tables for 1979-81," *Transactions of the Society of Actuaries*, XXXVII (1985). (With Francisco R. Bayo.)

11. "The Social Security Double-Indexing Myth," *Benefits Quarterly*, Third Quarter, 1986.

12. "Future Financing Problems of National Pension Systems Can Be Avoided, Automatically," *Proceedings, International Congress of Actuaries,* July 1988.

13. "The Undesirability of General Revenue Financing in the Social Security System of the United States," *Proceedings, International Congress of Actuaries*, July 1988.

14. "Social Security Funding Basis: Fiction and Fact," *Proceedings, of the Conference of Actuaries in Public Practice*, XXXVIII (1989).

15. "Real Wages Went Up in the 1980's," *The Wall Street Journal*, August 21, 1990.

16. "Early Retirement Reduction and Delayed Retirement Increase Factors under U.S. Social Security Law," (with Bruce D. Schobel), *Transactions of the Society of Actuaries*, XLII (1990).

17. "An Updated Money's-worth Analysis of Social Security Retirement Benefits," (with Bruce D. Schobel). To be published in *Transactions of the Society of Actuaries*, XLIV (1992).

18. *Social Security* (Fourth Edition). Philadelphia: University of Pennsylvania Press, 1992. (Originally published in 1965 by Richard D. Irwin, Inc., Homewood, Illinois.)

MEMBERSHIPS

Fellow, Society of Actuaries (President, 1971-72)

Fellow, Casualty Actuarial Society

Fellow, Conference of Consulting Actuaries

Fellow, Fraternal Actuarial Association

Member, American Academy of Actuaries (President, 1971-72)

Fellow, American Statistical Association

Fellow, American Association for the Advancement of Science

Fellow, Royal Statistical Society (Great Britain)

Corresponding Member, French Institute of Actuaries

Corresponding Member, Spanish Institute of Actuaries

Associate, Institute of Actuaries (Great Britain)

Member, International Actuarial Association
  (Vice President, 1975-77)

Member, International Association of Consulting Actuaries

Member, Inter-American Association of Social Security Actuaries
  (President, 1961-84)

Member, International Union for Scientific Study of Population

Member, Middle Atlantic Actuarial Club (President, 1957)

Member, Population Association of America
  (First Vice President, 1962)

Member, National Academy of Social Insurance
  (Board of Directors, 1986-)

AWARDS AND CITATIONS

Triennial Prize for Papers, Actuarial Society of America, 1941-43

Distinguished Service Award, United States Department of Health, Education, and Welfare, 1956

Career Service Award, National Civil Service League, 1959

Doctor of Laws, Muhlenberg College, 1964

Doctor of Laws, Lehigh University, 1970

Employee Benefits Man of the Year, *Pension and Welfare News*, 1974

Award of Merit, International Social Security Association, 1975

Distinguished Alumni Award, University of Iowa, 1980

Commissioner's Citation, Social Security Administration, 1982

Kudos of the Month, *50 Plus*, March 1982

Legion of Honor Bronze Medallion, Chapel of Four Chaplains, 1982

Distinguished Citizen Award, National Health and Welfare Mutual Life Insurance Association, 1983

Hall of Fame Award, Cheltenham High School, 1984

Certificate of Appreciation, Trust Territory of the Pacific Islands, 1986

Founders' Gold Medal, International Insurance Society, 1989

Award for Excellence, Temple University, 1990

Who's Who in America

Who's Who in the World

Contemporary Authors

REFERENCES

Articles and Reports

1. Lambro, Donald J., *Dollars and Sense.* National Taxpayers Union, Washington, D.C., February 1983.

2. *Report of the National Commission on Social Security Reform.* Washington: National Commission on Social Security Reform, 1983.

3. *Report to the President of the Committee on Economic Security* (with supplement). Washington: U.S. Government Printing Office, 1935.

4. *Social Security in America.* Washington: The Social Security Board (for the Committee on Economic Security), 1937.

Books

5. Allen, Frederick Lewis, *Since Yesterday.* New York: Bonanza Books, 1986.

6. Altmeyer, Arthur J., *The Formative Years of Social Security.* Madison: University of Wisconsin Press, 1966.

7. Dulles, Foster Rhea, *The United States Since 1865.* Ann Arbor: University of Michigan Press, 1969.

8. Hardy, Dorcas R. and C. Colburn Hardy, *Social Insecurity: The Crisis in America's Social Security System and How to Plan Now for Your Own Financial Survival.* New York: Villard Books, 1991.

9. Kelly, Alfred H. and Winfred A. Harbison, *The American Constitution: Its Origins and Development* (Fourth Edition). New York: W.W. Norton, 1970.

10. Light, Paul, *Artful Work: The Politics of Social Security Reform.* New York: Random House, 1985.

11. Manley, John F., *The Politics of Finance.* Boston: Little, Brown and Company, 1970.

12. Perkins, Frances, Foreword to *Development of the Social Security Act*, by E.E. Witte (see 15, below).

13. Reagan, Ronald, *An American Life.* New York: Simon and Schuster, 1990.

INDEX